A Future for Socialism

A FUTURE FOR SOCIALISM

John E. Roemer

Harvard University Press

Cambridge, Massachusetts
1994

This book has been digitally reprinted. The content
remains identical to that of previous printings.

Library of Congress Cataloging-in-Publication Data

Roemer, John E.
    A future for socialism / John E. Roemer.
      p. cm.
    Includes bibliographical references and index.
    ISBN 0-674-33945-2 (cloth)
         0-674-33946-0 (paper)
    1. Socialism. 2. Mixed economy. I. Title.
HX73.R625 1994
335—dc20   93-23208   CIP

Contents

Preface

The views held by all thoughtful people about socialism—how to sum up the historical experience of the twentieth century, what that experience implies about the future, if any, of socialism—have necessarily been radically transformed by the events of the last several years. Because these events are so fresh, there is a danger that one's thoughts about them are also half-baked. I feel doubly uneasy about putting my own thoughts into print after such a short while: in my past writings I have preferred to publish only statements that I could prove under sets of clearly stated axioms, but that approach is not possible for the present venture. Against these risks of publishing prematurely, one must balance the possible benefit of interjecting a different viewpoint in a vital debate while the iron is hot. Evidently, I have decided the expected net benefit is positive. I ask the reader, however, to take what is here with the spirit of inquiry in which it is offered.

I have made some effort to try to insure the reader against receiving shoddy goods: I have asked a number of friends and colleagues, whose judgment I trust, to read the manuscript, or parts of it, and share their criticisms with me. I am indebted to Samuel Bowles, G. A. Cohen, Joshua Cohen, Marc Fleurbaey, George Martin, William Simon, and Erik Wright for their detailed comments on the whole essay. I also thank Avner Ben-Ner, Fred Block, David Laitin, Andreu Mas-Colell, and Joaquim Silvestre for their comments on certain parts. Finally, I have borrowed liberally from my joint work with Pranab Bardhan, Ignacio Ortuño-Ortin, and Joaquim Silvestre, and I thank them for permitting me to publish our thoughts in this form.

A Future for Socialism

Introduction

The demise of the Communist system in the Soviet Union and Eastern Europe has bolstered old arguments, and created some new ones, that socialism cannot exist, either in the present world or as an ideal. I wish to argue that socialism remains an ideal worth pursuing and a possibility in the real world. The argument in favor of a socialist economy, as I see it, requires some revision of standard views of what constitutes socialism. Clearly the Soviet model of socialist society is dead, but that does not mean that other, untried forms of socialism should be buried along with it.

This essay is a defense of an alternative socialism, called market socialism. The term comes to us from the "socialist calculation" debate of the 1930s, whose principal protagonists were Oskar Lange and Friedrich Hayek. As I will summarize below (§4), Lange argued that what economists now call neoclassical price theory showed the possibility of combining central planning and the market, and Hayek retorted that planning would subvert at its heart the mechanism that gave capitalism its vitality. Hayek's criticisms of market socialism, and more recently those of Janos Kornai, are for the most part on the mark. But the experiences of capitalism, as well as of socialism, in the last fifty years suggest ways of reformulating the concept of market socialism in response to the Hayekian critique of its intellectual ancestor. My task in this essay is to propose and defend a new model that combines the strengths of the market system with those of socialism. Such a model would be concerned with both efficiency *and* equality.

Economic theory does not yet enable us to write a complete balance sheet of the benefits and costs of the market mechanism. During the 1930s, when Lange and Hayek wrote about market socialism, the Soviet Union was undergoing rapid industrialization. There was, apparently, full employment in that country, while workers and machines were massively idle in the industrialized capitalist world. Hayek therefore wrote from a defensive position, while Lange may well have felt that his proposal was simply a matter of fine-tuning for a socialist system that was, inevitably, the face of the future. Today, the tables are turned. Yet both the pro-socialists of the 1930s and the pro-capitalists of today jump too quickly to conclusions, for we understand fully the effects of markets only in very special circumstances.

Economic theory can explain how, if all economic actors are small relative to the market and cannot individually affect prices, if externalities are absent, and if there is a sufficient number of insurance and financial markets, a market economy will reach an equilibrium at which resources are allocated in a way that economists call Pareto-efficient— that is, efficient in the sense that no other allocation of resources exists which could render all people at least as well off and some people strictly better off.[1] But this kind of static efficiency may be unimportant relative to the dynamic efficiency with which markets are often credited—that they produce innovations in technology and commodities more effectively than any other economic mechanism could. Although we seem to have much evidence of market dynamism, we have no fully adequate economic theory of it: no one has ever produced a theorem proving that markets beat planning when it comes to innovation. Nor has a controlled experiment ever been done that would permit a skeptical scientist confidently to assert that markets are superior to planning in this dynamic sense. The real-life experiments are severely compromised, from a scientific viewpoint: the most dynamic economies of the last thirty years (Japan and the East Asian tigers) operated with both markets and a good dose of planning; in contrast, though the Communist economies had planning but no markets, they also had political dictatorship, a background condition that any experimental designer would like to be able to alter.

The economic theorist must, therefore, be much more agnostic about the effects of the market than are elementary economics textbooks and the popular press. Indeed, contemporary economic theory has come to see that markets operate within a context of nonmarket institutions. These are, notably, firms, contract law, the interlinking institutions between economic and other actors (such as between the firm and its stockholders), and the state. Large capitalist firms are centrally planned organizations (in which internal transactions are not mediated by a price system), and they are usually run by managers hired to represent the interests of shareholders. This they do imperfectly, as their own interests do not typically coincide with the interests of shareholders. Contract law is an essential supplement to the market: long-term contracts, in effect, render it costly for the parties to return to the market during the life of the contract. Furthermore, in different capitalist economies different kinds of nonmarket institutions have evolved—here, we do have somewhat of a real-life experiment that can help us evaluate alternative economic mechanisms. In Germany and Japan, for example, the institutions through which owners of firms monitor their managements are very different from those in the United States and Great Britain.

The market, in a word, does not perform its good deeds unaided; it is supported by a myriad cast of institutional characters that have evolved painstakingly over time, and in a variety of ways, in various market economies. This essay's central argument is that these institutional solutions to the design problems of capitalism also suggest how the design problems of socialism may be solved in a market setting.

To see why this may be so, I will first quickly, and necessarily inadequately, summarize the theory of income distribution of Hayek and of neoclassical economics. The distribution of income in a market economy, according to this view, is, in the long run, determined by the relative scarcity of various factors of production, principally human talents, including entrepreneurial talent. Property rights, although proximately related to income distribution, should in the long run be viewed as themselves derivative of talent. Firms are just the means through which entrepreneurs capitalize their talent; in turn, it is profits from firms which enable their owners to purchase real estate and other natural resources, which means that, in the long run, natural resources, too, are owned by talented people (or their descendants). Furthermore, any attempt to interfere with the operation of markets—that is, with the institution that maximizes the freedom to compete in the economic sphere—will, on this view, only reduce overall welfare, as it will inevitably inhibit entrepreneurs from bringing their talents fully into play.

Were this "naturalistic" view correct, egalitarians would have little remedy for inequality other than education, whose goal would be to develop the talents of as many people as possible, and perhaps inheritance taxes. But the advanced capitalist economy, as I described it above, is in large part the product of large, complex institutions, whose operation depends upon the combined efforts of many "ordinary" people—ordinary in the sense that their talents are not of the rare variety that must be given free rein in an environment of unrestrained competition; the talents of these economic actors may be instilled through training and education. The wealth of society is not due primarily to rugged individualists, as it were, but is reproducible according to blueprints that are quite well understood. The market is necessary to implement competition and to economize on information, but not so much for cultivating the inspiration of rare geniuses.

A particular way in which the modern view of capitalism suggests a future for socialism is in its understanding of the firm as a nexus of relationships between economic actors (in particular those that economists call principal-agent relationships, defined in §5). It is not correct to characterize modern capitalist firms as instruments by which entrepreneurs capitalize their talents. The profits of firms are distributed to many owners, all or a great many of whom have no direct control over decisions that affect profitability and are in large part not responsible for firms' successes or failures. Firms, in other words, are run by hired agents of their owners, and this suggests that hired agents could as well run firms in a socialist economy, one in which profits would be distributed even more diffusely than they are under capitalism. Indeed, the mechanisms that have evolved (or been designed) under capitalism that enable owners to control management can be transported to a socialist framework.

In contrast to the "thin" neoclassical view, which sees markets as a minimal structure organizing competition among talented individuals, the modern "thick" view sees markets as part of a complex network of man-made institutions, through which all individual contributions become pasteurized and refined. These two views of the market are, I suggest, substantially different, and the latter view, unlike the former, is amenable to the coexistence of markets and socialism. Income distribution, in particular, is more malleable under the modern view; the door is opened to the possibility of reducing inequality substantially, without having to wait for the results of massive education programs, as the reallocation of profits will, if properly done, have little or no deleterious effect on economic efficiency. The specific task of this essay is to suggest ways in which such a reallocation of profit income may be effected. I also hope to challenge an oft-cited criticism of market socialism: namely, that it is an oxymoron, that markets cannot perform their good deeds without the essentially unfettered right to private property in firms and the corollary right to accumulation of capital.

While the above paragraphs set the stage for what is to follow, it may also be useful to offer the reader a précis of the line of argument. I begin by discussing what I believe socialists want—the political philosophy, if you will, of socialism. Some liberals may be pleasantly surprised that I define socialism as a kind of egalitarianism; some socialists will be taken aback, for the notions of class and exploitation are not central to this egalitarian notion. In §2, I ask whether public ownership, as it has been conceived of in the socialist movement, is necessary to realize in a politico-economic system what socialists want. I answer that it is not. In particular, I claim that the direct control of firms by the state is not necessary for socialist goals; under monopoly conditions, it is positively harmful. Socialists should be eclectic in their attitude toward property relations: there may be many forms of ownership more amenable to socialism's goals than traditional state ownership of the means of production.

In §3, I distinguish between the short-term and long-term goals of socialism. Although the Bolshevik revolution appears to have failed, it placed in political discourse, in a way that millions could understand, the view that it is possible to organize society on egalitarian principles. Today, the long-term goals of socialism are being formulated by political philosophers; this essay attempts to formulate a short-term goal, that is, an economic mechanism capable of moving us closer to the ultimate goals. The fourth section provides a brief history of the idea of market socialism, including principally the contributions of Lange and Hayek, and notes how the idea has evolved continuously throughout the century. In the fifth section, I propose an explanation for why the centrally planned economies eventually failed: simply put, they were unable to solve principal-agent problems. Section 6 provides a sampling of seven contemporary models of market socialism, including ones based on labor-managed firms, ones based on profit-maximizing manager-run firms, and ones in which there is little explicit emphasis on property relations but rather more on other institutions.

Section 7 discusses how the levels of a number of "public bads" in a society, from pollution to imperialist wars, may be determined, through its political mechanism, by the way an economy distributes profits among its citizens. In particular, I argue that a reorganization of property rights in firms could significantly improve the "quality of life," as it is reflected in the absence of public bads, even before socialist values become widespread. This is, to my knowledge, a new argument in the theory of socialism. Section 8 studies a general-equilibrium model of market socialism.[2] In this section I argue that a stock market can be designed that does not seriously compromise egalitarianism while having beneficial effects on the efficiency of the economy.

Section 9 addresses specifically the issue that critics consider to be socialism's Achilles heel: How can a socialist economy—one in which the unfettered accumulation of profits by private citizens is banned—keep firms efficient and the pace of technological innovation brisk? The principal task is to design a device for monitoring the management of firms, one that does not depend upon the highly concentrated ownership of stock. Monitoring by public banks is proposed and defended, with reference to the recent literature in financial economics.

It has been argued by some that the economic failure of the Yugoslav economy in the 1970s is proof of the undesirability of market socialism. Section 10 provides a brief rebuttal to this claim, by arguing that the principal aspects of the model of market socialism defended here were absent in the Yugoslav experiment. Section 11 begins a discussion of investment planning and gives an example of how government intervention in the investment process can lead to socially superior outcomes. Section 12, which discusses investment planning, makes the point that planning may be carried out more effectively by the use of market instruments than by central commands and administrative allocation—thus, the failure of the Soviet-type command system is not an indictment of planning as such. A brief review of recent investment planning in Taiwan is offered as a successful example of the theory. Section 13 remarks on some consequences for socialist thinking of the desideratum of democracy. Realization of the goals of socialism will be a slow process, and the equalization of the distribution of profits will substantially change the character of democracy from its character under capitalism. Section 14 presents what I think are the most serious left-wing criticisms of market socialism. In the concluding remarks in §15, I try to balance the political realities of today's emerging economies with a sense of hope for the future.

§1

What socialists want

I believe socialists want equality of opportunity for:

(1) self-realization and welfare,
(2) political influence, and
(3) social status.

Self-realization is the development and application of an individual's talents in a way that gives meaning to life. This is a specifically Marxist conception of human flourishing.[1] It is to be distinguished, for instance, from philosopher John Rawls's notion of fulfillment of a plan of life, for a plan of life might consist in enjoying one's family and friends, or eating fine meals, or counting blades of grass.[2] These activities, however, do not count as self-realization, a process of self-transformation that requires struggle in a way that eating a fine meal does not. One does, however, derive welfare from enjoying one's family and eating fine meals, and so I do attribute value to these activities in the socialist's reckoning.[3]

That equality of *opportunity* for self-realization and welfare is the goal, rather than equality of self-realization and welfare, requires comment. Were equality of welfare the goal rather than equality of opportunity for welfare, then society would be mandated to provide huge resource endowments to those who adopt terribly expensive and unrealistic goals. Suppose I, a poor athlete, come to believe that my life will have been worthless unless I reach the top of Mount Everest on foot. It would require a large amount of money, to hire sufficient sherpas and other support services, to make that journey possible. Calling for equality of opportunity for welfare, on the other hand, puts some responsibility on me for choosing welfare-inducing goals that are reasonable.

It is certainly tricky to decide what allocation of resources will give all people an equal opportunity for welfare or self-realization, but I hope the principle is clear from this example. What distinguishes socialists or leftists from conservatives is, in large part, the matter of deciding what exactly is required to equalize opportunities. Conservatives believe that if there is no discrimination in hiring and everyone has access to education through a public school system or vouchers, then the standard of equality of opportunity is met. Socialists believe that those guarantees only touch the surface of a much larger task. Equality of opportunity requires special compensation or subsidy for those denied access to privilege. Most generally, equality of opportunity requires that people be compensated for handicaps induced by factors over which they have no control. If one believes that people never exercise free will, that all behavior is induced by factors beyond a person's control, then equality of opportunity for welfare collapses into equality of welfare. But most socialists and others believe that there is a realm for will, and hence it is important to insert the opportunity clause in any list of "what socialists want."[4]

Suppose that we have clarified what each item of the list

means—and I will not here attempt to offer any explication of (2) and (3). The statements are still inaccurate. For instance, what socialists really want is not equality of opportunity for self-realization, but equality of such at a high level. So (1) should be restated to read: Socialists want an organization of society that equalizes the opportunity for self-realization at a level no lower than that any other organization of society could achieve for everyone. Or, in other words, (1) says we should maximize, over all possible organizations of society, the level of opportunity for self-realization that *can* be achieved as an equal level for all. Desideratum (2) calls on us to choose that organization of society which maximizes the degree of equality for opportunity for political influence, and a similar statement holds for (3). It is, however, impossible to maximize three objectives at once. That is, the kind of social organization that maximizes the equal level of opportunity for self-realization may well induce highly unequal levels of political influence.[5]

There are two responses to this problem. The first says: There is a form of society in which all three objectives are equalized simultaneously, when "the free development of each becomes the condition for the free development of all," or some such thing. I think this is an unsubstantiated and utopian claim. The second response says that one must admit the possibility of trade-offs among the three objectives. This, in fact, is what most of us do. For instance, a lively debate has taken place in the socialist movement on the question, Which is primary, democracy or equality? Or, rephrased, Is equality of opportunity for political influence more important that equality of opportunity for self-realization and welfare? Socialists have different answers to this question. For example, western socialists assign more importance to equality of opportunity for political influence than most Soviet socialists did. Some socialists did not support the Sandinistas because of the lack of press freedom and democracy in Nicaragua.

To put the problem slightly more formally, imagine that we can rate each possible organization of society with a triple of numbers (a,b,c) where a is the degree of equality of opportunity for self-realization and welfare, b is the degree of equality of opportunity for political influence, and c is the degree of equality of opportunity for social status with that organization. What socialists disagree about is the preference ordering over all the possible combinations: Is an organization yielding levels $(2,1,3)$ better than one yielding $(1,2,3)$?

I shall not argue for one particular preference ordering, for I think that, at this time, there is a more urgent task. With the demise of what used to be called "actually existing socialism," the world has no model of any "feasible socialism"; indeed, many people have concluded that no such model exists. Until viable models are put forward, arguing about differences in preference orderings of the three desiderata is of second-order importance. Of course, in evaluating the desirability of various models that may be put forth, each of us will choose, for the meanwhile, a "personal" preference ordering.

I should remark that I am not sure whether, once equality of opportunity for self-realization, welfare, and political influence have been realized, equality of opportunity for social status need be appended as a desideratum. One may, that is, want equality of opportunity for social status only insofar as one believes that it facilitates the first two kinds of equality.[6] Put in Marxist terms, Is a classless society desirable for reasons other than achieving (1) and (2)? Alternatively, is equality of political influence necessary once equality of social status has been achieved? I don't know, so I will leave these as open questions.

Some socialists, and many Marxists, will strenuously deny that I have accurately portrayed here "what socialists want." They will say that what *they* want is the end of the system in which a small capitalist class lives off the surplus value that workers create and that is rightfully theirs—an end, that is, to exploitation. What I have put forth, they will say, is a liberal egalitarian creed, not a socialist—or a Marxist—one. I have argued, in earlier writings, that the ethical condemnation of capitalism that should be taken to lie at the foundation of the Marxist charge of exploitation is, in fact, one based on the unjust inequality of distribution of ownership rights in the means of production.[7] I therefore see the kind of egalitarian philosophizing of this section not as an alternative to Marx's theory of exploitation but as one component needed to make it ethically cogent.

G. A. Cohen (1990b) has recently suggested a politico-historical explanation for why many socialist scholars, formerly content with the Marxist condemnation of capitalism based upon the expropriation of surplus value, now take political philosophy more seriously. It used to be approximately true, he writes, that the working class:

(1) constituted the majority of society,
(2) produced the wealth of society,
(3) were the exploited people in society, and
(4) were the needy people in society.

Furthermore, the working class:

(5) would have nothing to lose from revolution, whatever its upshot, and
(6) could and would transform society.

It is no longer a good approximation of reality to say the working class is characterized by features (1) through (4). The proletariat, those who own nothing but their labor power, no longer constitute a majority of advanced capitalist societies. Nor are the neediest (racial minorities, especially women among them, sections of the elderly, those on welfare and the unemployed) clearly members of the productive working class. Certainly (5) is false—the upshot matters, as the Communist experience shows—and even if the end result of a revolution would benefit workers, the costs of transition cannot be ignored, by them or by theorists of socialist transformation.[8]

An alternative ethical theory to egalitarianism can also be taken to underlie the condemnation of capitalism on grounds of exploitation: namely, that people deserve to have what they produce, and hence capitalism, which deprives those who do the producing of a part of what they produce, is a society based upon theft. This was, Cohen argues, perhaps the most prominent Marxist view; it could coexist peacefully with egalitarianism for a time, because of the approximate fact that the working class was coincidentally characterized as above. But with the divergence of the groups characterized by features (1) through (4) in modern capitalism, it becomes necessary to opt for one ethical theory or the other: do only those who produce wealth deserve to receive it, or should everyone receive wealth insofar as he or she has a right to self-realization and welfare? Furthermore, one must note that the thesis that workers are exploited because the wealth a person produces with her labor is rightfully hers—the thesis of self-ownership—is the prime postulate in the modern theory of libertarianism, as expounded by Robert Nozick (1974).

Libertarians use the postulate of self-ownership to deduce the injustice of redistributive taxation; those Marxists for whom self-ownership is the foundation of the attack on capitalism must therefore explain why they reject libertarianism's animosity toward the welfare state. Egalitarianism, however, taken as an ethical postulate, implies both a condemnation of capitalist exploitation, because it is based upon unjust inequality of ownership of the means of production, and support for the welfare state.

I am not saying that socialists should adopt the ethical theory that works best from the pragmatic viewpoint, let us say, of justifying calls for socialist transformation in today's world. My argument, rather, is that one of the ethical theories that is used is wrong, the one based upon self-ownership. Modern egalitarian theorists (whom I briefly discuss in §3) have argued definitively that the thesis of self-ownership is not a justifiable ethical stance. People do not deserve to profit differentially from the luck of the birth lottery, which distributes valuable assets (talents, citizenship, parents) in an arbitrary and highly unequal way. The only sound ethical argument for socialism is an egalitarian one.

§2

Public ownership

Marx located the injustice of capitalism in exploitation, and the source of exploitation in private ownership of the means of production (MP). (There are different opinions concerning whether Marx viewed capitalism as unjust or whether, for him, justice was so much "bourgeois cant."[1] I take the view that, whatever he believed, his argument shows that capitalism is unjust.) He also identified private ownership of the MP as the cause of another unattractive feature of capitalism: its tendency to go through periods of crisis. The Marxist prescription was, therefore, to abolish the doubly guilty private ownership of the MP, and this prescription was interpreted by Lenin and the Bolsheviks to require state ownership of the MP. State ownership, in turn, has come to be known as public ownership by most of the world.

What *should* public ownership of an asset mean?[2] That the people have control over the disposition of that asset and its product. Myriad problems arise when one tries to assess whether a particular mechanism of popular decisionmaking in fact empowers the people in such matters; I shall conventionally say that democratic elections in an environment with ample civil liberties constitute popular decisionmaking. Obviously, the democratic process makes public ownership of an asset a rather weak concept, since the public can relinquish its control of an asset, through elections, in a variety of ways. For instance, in Eastern Europe, many different proposals for what to do about the formerly state-owned firms are currently under debate. Some advocate a distribution of ownership of firms to the people through the dispensation of vouchers; some would sell the assets to the highest private bidder; some favor self-management by workers, others traditional state ownership; still others want to turn the factories over to those who know most about the firms, the management and former *nomenklatura*. Any of these solutions might be chosen by democratic elections, in which case public ownership would voluntarily pass into some other form of ownership; that is, control of the means of production would be granted to some person or group.

Or consider the following: the government distributes a portfolio of stock in the nation's firms to each young adult at age twenty-one and permits the person to trade that stock as she wishes during her life; she would collect the dividends that her portfolio entitles her to, but she would be forbidden to cash in any stock. At death, her portfolio returns to the public treasury. Does this arrangement constitute public ownership of the MP? Who controls the disposition of the MP in this case? At some level, the public does, through the granting of portfolios to individuals and the collection of them at death. But during their lives, citizens would have the power, at least collectively, to influence firms to maximize profits in a way that some might feel resembles capitalism too much to be called public ownership: citizens would exercise their influence through selling stock when they thought the firm had poor profit prospects, which might force the firm to cut wages, lay off workers, or take other actions identified with capitalism.

My view is that socialists have made a fetish of public ownership: public ownership has been viewed as the *sine qua non* of socialism, but this judgment is based on a false inference. What socialists want are the three equalities I enumerated in §1; they should be open-minded about what kinds of property rights in the MP would bring about those three equalities. An infinite gradation of possible property rights separates full, unregulated private ownership of firms (which exists almost nowhere) and complete control of a firm by a government organ. There is no guarantee that the state-control end of this spectrum is optimal for bringing about the three equalities, nor is it guaranteed that any particular democratically chosen arrangement will bring about the three equalities. The link between public ownership and socialism is tenuous, and I think one does much better to drop the requirement that "the people" own the means of production from the socialist constitution. Socialists should want those property rights that will bring about a society that best promotes equality of opportunity for everyone. One cannot honestly say, at this point in history, that one knows what those property rights must be.

Another instance of the fetishism of public ownership is the position common among socialists that the public should decide, presumably through some kind of representative democracy, how to use the economic surplus (or, as economists say, how to determine the rate and sectoral distribution of investment). I shall, momentarily, agree with this conclusion, but not for the conventional reason offered by socialists. That conventional reason is that, since the workers produce the surplus, they should decide how it is used. But I do not view popular or political control over investment as a right, as that reason implies. It is important, but only for two reasons: in a market economy, the markets required to allocate investment efficiently do not exist, and investment has a number of external effects (more properly called externalities, a negative example of which is pollution) that are not well managed with markets. The missing markets are called futures markets.[3] To state the contrapositive, if there were a full set of futures markets, if externalities associated with investment were small, and if people's preferences were formed under conditions of equal opportunity, I would have little objection to determination of investment by the market, that is, by citizens in the economy determining the rate of investment as a consequence of individual responses to prices and interest rates.

What are some of the externalities associated with investment? First, investment determines future consumption, which will in part be enjoyed by people who do not yet exist. Their preferences are not expressed in markets today. The present generation must act as agents for tomorrow's consumers; clearly, this engenders a conflict of interest, even though the current generation cares about future generations. Because of this conflict of interest, political debate over the rate of investment is a good thing, for it will bring forward the position of those who feel most keenly their role as agents for future generations. Second, investment, which is naturally embodied in new technologies, requires more highly educated workers and thus encourages more training of workers. Training, and education in general, is a private, positive externality of investment for those who receive it; it is also a public good, insofar as a more highly educated population brings about a more cultured society.[4]

Thus, political control of the investment process, which I think *is* important, is so not because those who produced the surplus have the right to allocate it, but because market failures of a conventional kind make it preferable. Even if the surplus were not produced by today's workers, but, let us hypothetically say, by machines owned by one person, its allocation should not be left solely to markets, for the reasons just reviewed.

A category of property that deserves special mention is what William Simon (1991) has called social-republican property. This is private property owned by individuals but subject to two kinds of constraint: that "the holder bear a relation of potential active participation in a group or community constituted by the property, and [that] inequality [be limited] among the members of the group or community" (p. 1336). Simon shows that there exist a wide variety of property rights in the United States and other capitalist economies that satisfy these two conditions, which normally translate, in the law, into limitations on the right of transfer and the right to accumulate. An early example is the Homestead Act (1869), which bestowed ownership of land on a person subject to requirements that he settle, cultivate, and occupy it. The limitation, by social republicans, of ownership of property to those in proximity to it is meant to eliminate local public bads that absentee owners will produce if these bads increase the profitability of the property. It raises an important principle that I shall discuss further below (§7), that a form of property relation must be evaluated, *inter alia*, with respect to the kinds of public goods and bads it will engender.

Simon notes that citizenship and the right to vote are examples of rights that are not transferable and that cannot be accumulated, and one can argue that the rationale for the transfer prohibition, in both cases, is due to a public-bad effect. If votes could be sold, the poor would probably sell their votes to the rich, the result being that social and economic policy would be openly controlled by a small fraction of the population. The public-bad aspects of this arrangement are several, not least of which would be the severe alienation of the poor from their government. If citizenship could be sold, then a country would have fewer controls on the nature of its public culture, a public good presumably created by people with aspects of history and experience in common.[5] It is not surprising, then, that the same principle should extend to other kinds of property when public bads are an issue.

The labor-managed firm is perhaps the most well-known example of social-republican property, but there are many others. Rent control, which typically gives the renter security of tenancy at a controlled rent, is one. Note that the security of tenancy gives tenants the incentive to improve their property and community, that is, it engenders local public goods. (On the other hand, as is frequently noted, rent control may reduce the incentive of the landlord to improve the property.) Housing cooperatives are another instance. The Uniform Partnership Act in the United States makes key partnership rights nontransferable and provides, in the absence of contrary agreement, for equal division of profits among business partners.

In sum, I view the choice of property rights over firms and other resources to be an entirely instrumental matter; possibilities for organizing such rights should be evaluated by socialists according to the likelihood that they will induce the three equalities with which socialists are concerned. The history of socialism on the question is, very crudely, as follows: Private property, characteristic of capitalism, was under socialism declared to be public property, which became, under the Bolsheviks, state property. For complex reasons (including bureaucratic ossification and class interest), this form of ownership remained dominant for seventy years. The labor-managed firm remained a peripheral form of ownership in the socialist movement. The widest variety of property forms became visible in modern capitalism, not socialism: nonprofit firms, limited-liability corporations, partnerships, sole proprietorships, public firms, social-democratic property,[6] labor-managed firms, and other forms of social-republican property. The property forms that will best further socialist goals may involve direct popular control or state control of the means of production in only a distant way.

§3

The long term and the short term

The Bolshevik revolution was, I think, the most important political event since the French revolution, because it made real to hundreds of millions or perhaps billions of people, for the first time since 1789, the dream of a society based on a norm of equality rather than a norm of greed. Ludwig von Mises, no friend of socialism, wrote that the socialist movement was "the most powerful reform movement that history has ever known, the first ideological trend not limited to a section of mankind but supported by people of all races, nations, religions, and civilizations."[1] However we evaluate the results of the Bolshevik revolution, I think it would be a great mistake to underestimate the influence it had as a serious attempt at realizing that dream. Socialist and Communist parties formed in every country. I cannot evaluate the overall effects of these parties in organizing workers politically and in unions, in the antifascist struggle of the 1930s and 1940s, and in the postwar anticolonial struggle. It may well be that the advent of the welfare state, social democracy, and the end of colonialism are due, through this genesis, to the Bolshevik revolution.[2]

25

The Bolshevik revolution put both long-term and short-term proposals on the world's agenda. The long-term proposal was the formation of a classless society. The short-term proposal was a particular path of economic and social development, one that eschewed private ownership of the means of production. Today, for billions of people, no long-term or short-term socialist proposals are visible. The Right argues that no such proposals are possible: there was only one short-term proposal, the Communist system, and that has ingloriously and definitively failed. And, lacking a short-term proposal, it is pointless to dream of long-term ones that are any different from those promised by capitalism. Of course this view is myopic and unscientific: what has failed is one particular experiment, which occupied a very short period in the history of mankind. Nevertheless, to the extent that the Left succumbs to the myopic view, the development and implementation of new proposals will be all the more difficult.

The most important work today concerning what the long-term proposal of socialists should be is that of political philosophers on egalitarian theories of justice. Some socialist philosophers are at the forefront of this work, for example G. A. Cohen of Oxford University and Richard Arneson of the University of California at San Diego.[3] But other philosophers and political theorists, less identified with socialism, are also on the forefront: John Rawls, Ronald Dworkin, Amartya Sen, Brian Barry, and Thomas Nagel,[4] to name the most prominent. These scholars study the kinds of equality that are required for justice and the nature of the trade-offs one should be willing to accept among them. This work was not initiated by the socialist movement but by the publication of John Rawls's book, *A Theory of Justice*, in 1971. This book accomplished the feat of convincing a large number of social scientists that egalitarianism was not simply a "value judgment" that people might or might not hold according to their taste but was, rather, a view of what social arrangements were right, a view that any rational, honest person had to accept. Through these academics, many more millions will eventually be influenced, as these ideas are examined in the classroom and as they make their way into popular culture and policymaking.[5]

There is much debate today in the West, unfortunately less in the East, about what the short-term socialist goal should be. I believe that goal is some kind of market socialism. I think that any complex society must use markets in order to produce and distribute the goods that people need for their self-realization and welfare. It is much less clear that a market economy is compatible with equality of opportunity for political influence and equality of social status. As a short-term goal, market socialism may take form as any of a variety of economic arrangements in which most goods, including labor, are distributed through the price system, and the profits of firms, perhaps managed by workers or not, are distributed quite equally among the population. I shall go into more detail later; but first, I think it will be useful to present a short history of the idea of market socialism.

§4

A brief history of the idea of market socialism

For a history of the idea of market socialism up until 1940, one can hardly do better than read Friedrich Hayek (1935, 1940) and Oskar Lange (1956).[1] In 1940 Hayek characterized the debate as having entered its third stage with the publication of Lange's famous paper "On the economic theory of socialism." The first stage was marked by the realization by socialists that prices must be used for economic calculation under socialism; accounting in some kind of "natural unit," such as the amount of energy or labor commodities embodied, simply would not work. The second stage was characterized by the view that it would be possible to calculate the prices at which general equilibrium would be reached in a socialist economy by solving a complicated system of simultaneous equations—and so socialism need only await the invention of powerful computers. Hayek attributed this view to H. D. Dickinson, although Dickinson retracted it in his *Economics of Socialism* (Oxford, 1939), written approximately contemporaneously with Lange (1936). The third stage was marked by the realization, by Lange and others, that actual markets would indeed

28

be required to find the socialist equilibrium—and this because the central planning bureau could not possibly have the information necessary to make the calculation, as the information needed—for instance, on how much each consumer would be willing to pay for each good—would be too massive ever to compile.

Lange's proposal was, very briefly, as follows. Prices of consumer goods would be determined by the market, and wages would be determined by the market and be augmented by whatever institutions for wage bargaining existed. The rate of investment or accumulation would be set by the central planning bureau (CPB). Prices of industrial goods would be determined by a kind of *tâtonnement* procedure, or estimation by "groping," conducted by the CPB. After the CPB announced its candidates for industrial prices, firm managers would be mandated to calculate their output using two rules: to choose that production technique which minimized unit costs at those prices, and to choose the level of output by setting marginal cost equal to price.[2] If all technologies were characterized by constant or decreasing returns to scale (if, in other words, increasing the input to the production process by a factor increases the output only by the same or even a smaller factor),[3] the firms should "choose output to maximize profits at going prices." Managers would then report their input demands and output supplies, at these prices, to the CPB. The center would then propose a new vector of candidate prices, in which prices were raised for goods in excess demand and lowered for goods in excess supply. In addition, the center would set the interest rate on capital to reach, at equilibrium, a target rate of accumulation.

Within the stylized assumptions of the model, there are two obvious questions to ask about this proposal: Is there any guarantee that the estimations in the *tâtonnement* procedure would ever "converge" and produce an equilibrium price vector and, if so, how fast? And what is the region of rates of accumulation that indeed can be supported by equilibria of such a model? The first question was studied by Kenneth Arrow and Leonid Hurwicz (1960), although the modern skepticism on the convergence of *tâtonnement* received its firm foundation later in the work of Hugo Sonnenschein (1973) and Gérard Debreu (1974).[4] The second question has been studied only recently, by Ortuño, Roemer, and Silvestre (1993), and is the topic of §12 below. A third question generated by the model has only recently received a complete study (see, for example, Quinzii, 1992): if some firms have increasing returns to scale, when will there exist a "marginal-cost pricing equilibrium" and what are its efficiency properties?

But fifty years ago these "within-the-model" questions were not asked. The trenchant attack on the Lange model claimed that its assumptions were missing fundamental aspects of a complex economy. Hayek's (1940) main attack is against Lange's *tâtonnement* procedure on several grounds: first, that *tâtonnement* will not converge, because at each step of the procedure the world will have changed, and so the target will be forever a moving one and managers will be changing, at each step, the set of feasible technologies they choose from (for instance); second, that commodities are incredibly complex things, and hence it would be impossible for the CPB even to name the many prices that efficient resource allocation via a market system requires; and third, that even were such a list presented, the procedure would preclude even loyal and capable firm managers from finding the least-cost production methods.

Hayek claims that Lange never justifies disallowing market determination of industrial prices in his proposal along with consumer goods' prices and wages. Indeed, Lange actually does, but the justification seems weak if not wrong. He says that disequilibrium in industrial prices is very costly to the economy, since these prices determine the prices of all other goods, and that the CPB can find the equilibrium faster than the market can! I am puzzled by this. It seems that perhaps Lange feared that, were he to allow the market to determine all prices in his model (except the interest rate), he would be giving up too much and would lose credibility among socialists. As Hayek notes (1940, p. 130), the Lange proposal already makes great concessions to those who opposed pervasive planning; perhaps Lange believed it would not have been politically wise to go further.

But if the setting of industrial prices by the CPB is, as Hayek himself suggests, an expendable part of Lange's proposal, what are Hayek's essential attacks on Lange? Equivalently, suppose that Lange had allowed the market to determine both industrial and consumer prices, once the CPB set the interest rates (for instance) to achieve the desired rate of accumulation. (See Ortuño, Roemer, and Silvestre, 1993, for details.) What criticisms would Hayek then have leveled against the proposal? From his 1940 paper, there appear to be several possibilities. The first would again emphasize the decentralization of private information, which would make it impossible for the CPB to set any parameters (such as interest rates) to realize a given target.[5] The second is that, to the extent the planners would require anything (other than profit maximization) of the firm managers, the managers could not then be held responsible for losses the firms incurred; thus, any interference with the market by the CPB would let the manager off the hook and, in effect, place all responsibility on the planners for the outcome. This point brilliantly foreshadows the political sociology of the soft budget constraint as developed by Janos Kornai (e.g., 1992, 1993) some thirty years later.[6] The third criticism—and here Hayek attacks Dickinson more specifically than Lange—is that the planning authority in a socialist state could not help but interfere with the natural process of competition in many ways; it would impose its "paternalistic" views concerning not only the choice between present and future consumption but also, for example, the relative size of public and private consumption. Thus, freedom would gradually be usurped, and "socialism is bound to become totalitarian." At least the first two criticisms are treated seriously in the conception of market socialism I describe in §§8 and 9.

To continue Hayek's enumeration, we might say that the fourth stage in the development of the idea of market socialism was associated with the period of market reforms in the Communist countries: notably, Yugoslavia after 1950; Hungary after the New Economic Mechanism was introduced in 1968; China with the decollectivization of agriculture and other subsequent reforms, beginning in 1978; Poland between 1981 and 1989; and the Soviet Union in the Gorbachev period, starting in 1985. These experiments were certainly not perfect ones, in the sense that nowhere were prices as free as the (revised) Lange model would have required, nowhere was competition allowed to determine the fate of state firms, nor anywhere were domestic firms forced to compete in the international market. (A characterization of the essential economic and political characteristics of these experiments is found in Kornai, 1993.)

One of the main intellectual contributions of the period is Kornai's theory of the soft budget constraint, which further articulates Hayek's point that central planners who interfere with the market cannot then hold firms responsible for losses and which explains the precise forms that this problem takes: the myriad loans, "soft" prices, and "soft" taxes that were manipulated to keep afloat firms which, without such intervention, would have failed. Kornai's central point is that, knowing such rescues are always on the way, firm managers fail to take seriously any instructions from the center; financial control of firms by the center thereby becomes impossible, as managers do not treat parametrically any prices, taxes, or other measures that are announced. Besides, the selection, promotion, and dismissal of firm managers depend more on political loyalty to party bosses than on the firm's economic performance.

Other significant contributors to the fourth-generation debate were Wlodzimierz Brus (1972) and Alec Nove (1983). But perhaps the main contribution to the debate in this period was made by authors who were not explicitly concerned with market socialism: this was the formulation and study by economic theorists of the concept of incentive compatibility. The theory of incentive compatibility situated the soft-budget-constraint problem as a special case of a vastly more general problem: that planners, in issuing directives to firm managers, must design incentives so that following the rules is in the best interest of the managers. This need not imply that managers' sole interests are in personal financial remuneration; it means, rather, that management cannot be expected to do X when doing Y will improve more than X the manager's career prospects, the success of the firm, or other goals.

The fifth stage of the market-socialism debate is the present one. Not only have the proponents of market socialism retracted Lange's insistence that industrial prices be set by the planners instead of the market, but they have also dispensed with public ownership (in the sense of exclusive state control) of firms. In these proposals, some of which I will briefly describe below in §6, firms are envisaged as operating independently of state control, with boards of directors representing either workers or various institutions (banks, mutual funds, pension funds) that hold stock in the firms or are responsible for its financing. Kornai's and Hayek's point has been accepted, that as long as the government cannot credibly commit itself to noninterference in the competitive process, managers will not be profit-maximizers and economic inefficiency will result. A credible commitment can best be created by retracting the state's power to interfere in the management of the firm and establishing some binding arrangements to ensure competition (particularly international competition).

But if public ownership in the usual sense has now been dropped as a prerequisite, by what lights do these fifth-generation models deserve to be called models of socialism? The essential point is that firms are not, in these models, held as private property either. Denationalization does not imply privatization: there are a number of different kinds of property rights that would, the argument goes, induce firm managers to maximize profits—at least about as effectively as they do in large capitalist corporations—but that would also preclude profits from being distributed among citizens in the extremely unequal way characteristic of capitalism. These proposals trace their claim to socialism, then, to the relatively egalitarian distribution of profits they hope to implement and to their abrogation of the right to the massive accumulation of private property in the means of production. They also variously call for more planning than exists in most (but not all) capitalist countries today, most especially with regard to investment. In terms of the initial wish list of socialists, these proposals are concerned mainly with implementing a more equal distribution of income, by preventing growth of a small class whose members derive huge incomes from the profits of firms. Proponents of these mod-

els hope that equality of opportunity for political influence
and equality of social status will thereby be enhanced, although, in the long run, these and more equality in the
distribution of income will require, I think, a massive increase in the resources devoted to education (on which more
below in §13).

As I have outlined, with Hayek's help, the five stages in
the development of the idea of market socialism, it may
appear that the socialists have made all the concessions—
and that this fifth stage will be the last, to be followed by the
universal recognition, some ten or thirty or fifty years hence,
that only a system of conventional capitalist private ownership yields a satisfactory combination of dynamic efficiency,
equity, and freedom. I take issue with this view. For capitalism, also, has made major concessions to socialism during
the last century.

First, despite the experience of the past decade, the share
of the public sector has grown sharply over time in capitalist
countries, a reflection of the reality that a laissez-faire private ownership regime is politically unacceptable, at least
under democratic conditions. (Think not only of the increase in the share of public investment but also of the
welfare state.)

Second, what almost all would consider the social and
economic success of the Nordic social democracies attests
to the possibility of substantially altering the distribution of
income in a capitalist country toward equality without un-
acceptably dulling the incentives for profit maximization.
Put slightly differently, a degree of freedom exists in the
distribution of income, subject to an acceptable lower bound
on efficiency, that the "naturalist" view of Hayek and the
Austrians would deny.

Third, the East Asian development "miracles" of the
postwar period show the possibility of extensive govern-

ment intervention in the economy without relieving firm owners and managers of the discipline of competition. Here, indeed, governments succeeded in making credible the commitment that firms (even state-owned ones, as in Taiwan and South Korea) would not be rescued if, for instance, they failed to succeed in international competition.

Fourth—and this is not a concession of capitalism to socialism but an argument for the feasibility of nonprivate ownership—advanced corporate capitalism has proved that complex principal-agent problems in the management of firms can be solved, agency problems that are perhaps no less complex than the kind a firm would face in the fifth-generation proposals of market socialism.

In addition, the theory of capitalism has made concessions to socialist critiques in the realm of economic theory: it is widely accepted that there can exist unemployment at equilibrium in capitalist economies; that market equilibria may be suboptimal because of missing markets, coordination failures, and externalities; and that, in particular, market-determined rates of investment may be suboptimal.

§5

Why the centrally planned economies failed

The failure of the Soviet-type economies was due to the conjunction of three of their characteristics: (1) the allocation of most goods by an administrative apparatus under which producers were not forced to compete with each other, (2) direct control of firms by political units, and (3) noncompetitive, nondemocratic politics. Identifying these features as the cause, however, does not *explain* the failures, for we must uncover the mechanism through which they inhibited economic development. In the previous section, I alluded to principal-agent problems as a serious problem for the Soviet-type economies. A principal-agent problem arises when one actor (a principal) must engage another (the agent) to perform a task. In general, the agent has interests which differ from the principal's, and if the principal cannot easily monitor or supervise the agent, then the agent will not do just what the principal wants done. Such problems arise everywhere in economic life, and economic theory has devoted much effort to analyzing them in the last twenty years.

I believe, however, that the true explanation of the demise

of Soviet-type economies is somewhat more complex. Indeed, I now think that I have assigned the wrong weight to these principal-agent problems in some of my own recent work (Roemer, 1992a). In this section I shall first outline an argument that principal-agent problems caused the failure of the Soviet-type economies and then offer some criticisms and modifications of it.

The contour of the argument is that the three characteristics I just listed conspired to prevent the solution of principal-agent problems that, in capitalist democracies, are successfully solved. Communist societies faced principal-agent problems in three important types of relationship: between managers and workers in factories and collective farms, between government planners and firm managers, and between the public and the planners. Managers must try to get workers to carry out their production plans, planners must try to get managers to carry out the planning bureau's plan, and the planners, in a socialist regime, are supposed to be agents doing the best they can for their collective principal, the public.

The initial, utopian view of the Bolsheviks, and later of the Maoists in China, was that economic incentives were unnecessary to solve these principal-agent problems. A socialist society would instead rely upon the transformation of human values: idealists envisioned a society of selfless individuals working for the good of all, the model being what used to be called "socialist man." In Mao's lingo, all should learn to "serve the people" and to reject those actions which maximize personal security or comfort. If this transformation had occurred, the agency problems would have been greatly mitigated. In the event, most people could not motivate themselves, for a lifetime, by serving only the public good: people responded to their immediate situations much as they do in capitalist societies, by trying to look after their material interests a good proportion of the time.

To be more specific, the *manager-worker agency problem* festered for two reasons: workers had little motivation to work hard if it was virtually impossible to fire them, and there was little incentive to earn more because so few goods were available to buy. Much of the consumption bundle, including housing, was provided directly by the firm and not through the market. Second, the *planner-manager relationship* became one where the planners, or politicians, depended on the firms in their regions for income, and so, rather than carrying out plans proposed by the planning bureau, firm managers entered into bargaining relationships with politicians. An example of the kinds of problem this led to was the "soft budget constraint": political authorities extended loans and tax exemptions to firms that, from the viewpoint of economic efficiency, should not have been granted such extensions. These arrangements were allowed to continue in part because, in a system that did not officially recognize the existence of unemployment, there was no mechanism for retraining and rehiring laid-off workers, and also because fulfilling the plan's production quotas was often evaluated independently of the costs entailed in so doing. The path of least resistance for government and planning bureaucrats often consisted in continuing to finance a firm that should have been allowed to die. The third agency problem, between the planners and the public, was supposed to be solved, in theory, by the vanguard role of the Communist Party: "From the masses to the masses" was Mao's theory of the party as agent of the people. But Mao was wrong: political competition is required to empower the public, and competition was thoroughly squashed by Communist parties throughout the world holding state power.

What are the analogous principal-agent problems in a capitalist economy, and how are they addressed? The manager-worker problem remains essentially the same; it is solved by using both the carrot and the stick. Arguably, the carrot works better. For instance, job ladders within the firm, with wages increasing as one moves up the ladder, are constructed to give workers an incentive to build a career in the firm. This arrangement is explained by a type of "efficiency wage" theory, in which a firm pays a worker more than the worker is willing to accept—or, to be somewhat imprecise, more than the market requires—to bind her to the job. Much of modern industrial relations is concerned with ways of solving the manager-worker agency problem.

Under capitalism, the analogue of the planner-manager agency problem is the *stockholder-manager agency problem.* Managers are supposed to undertake policies that are in the best interest of the stockholders, that is, to maximize profits or the value of the firm. It is often not in the best personal interest of the manager to do so: he may not want to liquidate an unprofitable branch of the firm, because of the stress involved in laying off the employees; or he may be reluctant to distribute profits as dividends to shareholders, preferring to keep them to finance projects internally and thus to avoid the scrutiny that a bank would insist upon before approving a loan; or, he may purchase corporate jets for executive travel and make other lavish expenditures that are not in the stockholders' interest. Different capitalist economies have undertaken quite different strategies to solve this agency problem. It is believed by many finance economists that the stock market and the takeover process force managers to operate firms in the interests of shareholders. If profits decline because of bad management, the stock price of the firm falls and the firm becomes an attractive target for a takeover. The threat of takeover, it is argued, is the main disciplinary device that induces managers to act in the interests of shareholders.

Japan, however, appears to have a quite different way of creating efficient management. The stock market has been relatively unimportant in Japanese corporate finance. Firms are largely financed by bank loans, and stockholders have little say in corporate decisions.[1] Japanese firms are organized into groups called *keiretsu*, each of which is associated with a main bank that is responsible for organizing loan consortia for the firms in its group. The bank is in large part responsible for monitoring the firm's management. The bank even protects its firms from takeovers. A bank has an interest in running a tight ship so that its *keiretsu* is an attractive one for new firms to join, for if it disciplines unprofitable firms it can more easily arrange loan consortia for its *keiretsu*'s members.

What is the analogue of the public-planner agency problem under capitalism? It must be the *public-stockholder agency problem*, except neither property relations nor culture in the capitalist system require the stockholder to be an agent of the public. At this point, the theory of capitalism invokes Adam Smith: the actions taken by stockholders, that is to say firm owners, to serve their own interests are the same actions that turn out (unintentionally) to serve everyone's best interest—as though the stockholders were directed by an "invisible hand" to promote the public good. But the invisible hand only works well under a stringent set of conditions. In practice, modern capitalist societies have developed other institutions to step in where the invisible hand fails: antitrust law, regulation of various kinds, taxation and public expenditures, and so on.

The argument that principal-agent problems defeated the Communist states, then, seeks to establish that a combination of markets and political democracy solves capitalism's three principal-agent problems better than dictatorship and administrative allocation solve the three problems in Soviet-type economies.

The skepticism I now have about the validity of this argument is that, in the postwar period, from 1950 to 1970, the Soviet-type economies did quite well. Indeed, the Western attacks on these economies were of a markedly different nature from their attacks of the late 1980s. In the earlier period, Western critics of Communism argued that, *despite* its economic success, Communism was bad for human welfare because it deprived the people of political freedom.

During this period, the record on economic growth in the seven Comecon economies was about the same as in the eighteen countries of the Organization for Economic Co-operation and Development (OECD). Growth in output per worker in these countries in the period 1950–1967 averaged 4.1 percent per annum, while it averaged 4.0 percent per annum in the OECD countries.[2] If one compares labor productivity in countries at approximately the same level of development and culture, one gets a somewhat different story. In East and West Germany, labor productivity grew at 3.7 percent and 4.1 percent, respectively; in Hungary, labor productivity grew at 3.8 percent, and in Austria at 4.8 percent. These figures do indicate that growth, when normalized for culture and level of development, may have been somewhat higher—though not dramatically so—in the West.

Moreover, the economic growth in the East was perhaps more costly than in the West, in the sense of being purchased only with higher rates of investment. The average ratio of gross fixed investment to gross national product (GNP) in the period 1950–1966 in the Comecon countries was 24.7 percent, not markedly higher than the average rate of investment in the OECD countries, at 21.1 percent. If, however, one disaggregates the OECD countries and compares the record only of OECD countries at low levels of development (Turkey, Greece, Portugal, Japan, Ireland, Italy, and Austria) with the Comecon countries, one sees a somewhat different picture. The ratio of the investment rate to the GNP/worker growth rate in the Comecon countries was 6.9 percent in this period; in the low-development OECD countries, it was 4.2 percent. It thus appears that growth was more dearly purchased in the Comecom countries than in the capitalist countries at comparable levels of development.

Nevertheless, the economic growth record of the Communist economies was quite respectable during this period. Indeed, the rhetorical tone of Abram Bergson's article, written in 1971, and from which the above data are taken, is that OECD growth was *not inferior* to growth in the Communist economies, which indicates the perceptions of the time. It would be interesting, I think, to calculate the costs for growth of the nonmilitary sector sustained by virtue of the huge investment outlays that we now know were made for military purposes in the Soviet Union, and perhaps the other Comecom countries.

If, indeed, it is true that for about twenty years in the postwar period, and certainly during the 1930s in the Soviet Union, economic growth was respectable in the Communist economies, then we cannot simply invoke principal-agent problems as an explanation of the failure of those economies in the 1980s. At least, the principal-agent argument is not sufficiently fine-grained, for some characteristic of these economies that changed between 1960 and 1985 must be brought into play. I conjecture that what changed was the dependence of the growth in economic welfare on technological change. In the immediate postwar period, economic welfare could grow rapidly without technological innovation, since these economies were in large part devastated by World War II and rebuilding them increased economic welfare a great deal, even without technological innovation (so-called extensive growth). By the 1980s, or perhaps earlier, growth in economic welfare depended much more on the ability of an economy to innovate, to adopt new technologies producing improved commodities. At this, the Soviet-type economies failed dismally, and I think it is misleading to characterize this failure as one due to principal-agent problems, except in the tautological sense that the public was not being well served by its agents, the planners and managers, because the latter were not successful in introducing technological change.

To state the issue somewhat differently, it is false to say that sufficient technological change did not occur because some agent was not carrying out some principal's orders. No one gave such orders. The correct statement is that, without the competition that is provided by markets—both domestic and international—no business enterprise is forced to innovate, and without the motivation of competition, innovation, at least at the rate that market economies engender, does not occur. Perhaps even this view puts too much emphasis on the incentive question. It might just have been extremely difficult to innovate in the Soviet-type economies, because, for instance, information about commodities on the technological frontier was very hard to come by, because the best engineers and scientists were recruited by the defense sector, and because the system belittled the kind of consumer gratification that is catered to by capitalist enterprise. It thus becomes possible to explain why the Soviet economic system served people poorly even if managers and workers worked hard, as one sometimes hears was the case.[3] This view contrasts with the principal-agent explanation, which tends to emphasize the claim that managers and workers didn't work hard because they had no incentive to do so.

There are other explanations of the failure of Soviet-type economies in the period beginning in the late 1960s. Peter Murrell and Mancur Olson (1991) argue that, when political power is highly concentrated in the hands of a few (as under Stalin), then orders will be implemented more faithfully than when competing groups of political leaders and industrial lobbies emerge. Rent-seeking, as it were, increased in the Brezhnev period.[4] Ivan Major (1992) argues that Soviet-type economies suffered from periods of "exhaustion," of which the last twenty years was the worst. His argument, however, is unconvincing, as he fails to distinguish clearly between the characteristics of exhaustion and its causes. Others note the increasing complexity of the Soviet economy: Blackburn (1991, p. 40) notes that the Second Five Year Plan mentioned only about 300 specific products, whereas the 1960 plan dealt with 15,000 products produced by 200,000 enterprises. Jens Andvig (1992) proposes a model of bureaucratic organization, in which there can be both high-performance and low-performance equilibria. He argues that under Stalin the equilibrium was high-performance and under Brezhnev it was low-performance.

The question for socialists becomes, then, whether an economic mechanism can be designed under which technological innovation will take place but in which a characteristically capitalist distribution of income does not evolve. More specifically, can competition between business enterprises, leading to innovation, be induced without a regime of private property in the means of production? This question is vitally important, for, at this point, we have no observations of innovation as a generic, multisectoral phenomenon in an economy except when it is induced by competition.[5]

§6

Contemporary models of market socialism

In this sampling of models that reflect current thinking on the possibilities for a socialist future, I shall limit myself to proposals with two properties. First, the models must admit the extensive use of the market, for I think that any other proposal for the short term is simply utopian, for the reason discussed at the end of the preceding section. We know of no mechanism for inducing innovation on an economy-wide basis except market competition. Second, these proposals take people as they actually are today, not as they might be after an egalitarian economic policy or cultural revolution has "remade" them. We must assume, as social scientists, that people are, in the short term, at least, what they are: what can be changed—and slowly, at that—are the institutions through which they interact.

I shall discuss three types of proposal: proposals based on the idea of labor-managed firms, proposals for retaining traditional management forms but allowing for a more equal distribution of income, and proposals that do not envision a change in property rights as a central feature of the new system. There are many more proposals than the seven I have chosen to discuss: my choice is parochial in that six of the seven proposals I'll refer to appear in a recent book that I have co-edited with Pranab Bardhan (1993).

The biggest quandary concerning the feasibility of an economy consisting primarily of labor-managed firms (LMFs) is the financing problem. There are two reasons for maintaining that workers should not self-finance their firms: first, this would place both the worker's labor and financial assets in the same venture, a very poor diversification strategy in a risky world; second, it would relegate LMFs to that sector of the economy with small capital requirements per worker. Consider the dozen workers who are required to run a supertanker (see, for this example, Drèze, 1993). Even if they could borrow the money to buy the supertanker, using it as collateral, the riskiness of the business would, with large probability, bankrupt them. The monthly payments on the loan would be so large that the passage of a few months with no income, because of a decrease in oil sales internationally, would bring about foreclosure. Thus, with capital-intensive industries, it is necessary that someone other than the workers finance the firm.

The proposals of Jacques Drèze (1993), Marc Fleurbaey (1993), and Thomas Weisskopf (1993) all meet this problem by permitting external financing. Fleurbaey's LMFs are financed by bank loans, and the banks themselves are LMFs. Citizens can save in banks but cannot purchase equity in firms directly. Thus, banks would share control of a firm with its workers. In Weisskopf's proposal, LMFs would be financed by equity raised on a stock market. Citizens would be able to purchase shares of mutual funds, which in turn would purchase shares of firms. Mutual funds, however, would not have voting rights with their stock. Thus the firm would nominally be controlled only by its workers. I say nominally, because clearly a mutual fund can influence the investment policy of the firm by threatening to sell its stock. Drèze, who does not lay out a precise institutional proposal, notes that the workers of a firm would have to sign contracts with capital suppliers to share control over some decisions.

Some other aspects of traditional conceptions of the LMF are also modified by these proposals. Traditionally, the wage received by a worker is a share of the net revenues of the firm. It used to be thought that if LMFs acted to maximize net revenues per worker, Pareto-inefficiency would result at equilibrium. Such a scheme, Drèze (1989) has shown, does not lead to Pareto-inefficiency when there are capital suppliers who must be paid. But a scheme like this does imply that the worker's wage will vary with the fortunes of the firm. Most workers would rather be protected from such variation, and Drèze suggests a way of doing this. The wage should consist of two parts: a fixed part would be paid directly to the worker; and another part, which would vary with the firm's fortunes, would be invested in the national social security fund. In this way, the pensions of workers would be financed by a fund that bore only the aggregate risk of the economy, which is as good as one can hope for.

It is also noteworthy that LMFs might not maximize revenue per worker. For example, they might maximize the number of workers employed subject to a minimum income for workers—at least, this might be the objective during hard times. There has been no study of the efficiency properties of the equilibrium if all LMFs maximize employment subject to a floor on income.

The second type of market-socialist proposal retains the profit-maximizing firm, which is run by a manager chosen by a board of directors. This type is represented by proposals of Pranab Bardhan (1993) and myself. What renders them socialist is that individuals are not allowed to invest money in firms in the "public" sector, with a consequent

equalizing effect on the distribution of profits. Both proposals allow small private firms to exist. In Bardhan's proposal, the universe of public firms is partitioned into groups,
modeled after the Japanese *keiretsu*. The firms in each group
are associated with a main bank. The bank is responsible for
raising capital for the firms in its group and for monitoring
their managements. Firms in a group own shares of each
other; the dividends a firm receives from other firms are
distributed to its workers. Bardhan's purpose is to design a
mechanism for solving the problem of the soft budget constraint, which plagued the Eastern European and Soviet
economies. He argues that his system would produce the
right incentives: the other firms in a group and the main
bank would see to it that any given firm pursues a profit-
maximizing strategy. (See §9 for more details.) The Bardhan corporate structure is intended as an answer to those
who argue that only firms with highly concentrated ownership, as one finds under capitalism, will be monitored
successfully, for only a shareholder who stands to lose millions if the firm runs poorly will have the incentive to hold
the whip over management.

In my proposal, firms are also financed by loans from
public banks, which are responsible for monitoring firm
management. The profits of firms, however, are distributed
to individual shareholders. Initially, the government distributes a fixed number of coupons or vouchers to all adult
citizens, who use them to purchase the stock of firms, denominated not in regular currency but in coupons. (A more
elaborate discussion of this model is the subject of §§8 and
9, below.) Owning a share of a firm entitles the citizen to a
share of the firm's profits. More realistically, citizens may
invest their coupons in shares of mutual funds, which purchase shares of firms. One cannot purchase shares or coupons with money. People, however, can trade shares in firms

for shares in other firms, at coupon prices. Thus, prices on the coupon stock market will oscillate as they do on a regular stock market.

Because money cannot be used on the coupon stock market, the small class of wealthy citizens will not end up owning the majority of shares. And because concentration of ownership of firms in a small class is thereby prevented, I argue that economic policy in such an economy would be significantly different from capitalist economic policy, even if the capitalist economy began also with an equal division of shares of firms. Furthermore, the coupon stock market should provide the same discipline over firm management as a capitalist stock market does. When banks see the coupon share price of a firm falling, that is a sign that investors think the firm is performing poorly, and the banks would step in to monitor closely the management. Everyone's coupon portfolio would be returned to the public treasury at death, and allocations of coupons would continually be made to the new generation of adults. Thus, the coupon system is a mechanism for giving people a share of the economy's total profits during their lifetimes while also harnessing what good properties the stock market has as a device for risk-bearing and monitoring of firms.

As long as a market for labor exists, and people are differentially educated and talented, there will be wage differentials. The Bardhan and Roemer proposals concentrate on equalizing the distribution of that other part of national income, profits. Some proponents of LMFs believe that wage differentials would be limited to 3 or 4.5 to 1, based on the experience of Mondragon, Spain, the place where worker-controlled firms have been most widely introduced.

I think the principal weakness of the managerial-firm proposals is that firms would not be democratically run. Although income would be more equally distributed, the relationship of the worker to her firm may not change much. (Of course, there is a great deal of possible variation in this relationship under capitalism, as in Japan and the United States.) The principal advantage of this model is that it involves probably the smallest change from actually existing capitalism, and therefore it perhaps has the largest probability of running as efficiently as capitalism does.

The principal strength of the LMF proposals is that they change the relationship between workers and firms. The weaknesses are that, without profit-maximization, it is less clear that the economy would remain on the cutting technological edge. It is also not well understood to what extent giving firms access to the capital market, as the three LMF proposals I have reviewed advocate, would compromise the control of the firms by workers.

The third class of proposals, represented by those of Fred Block (1992) and Joshua Cohen and Joel Rogers (1993), does not envisage a *de jure* change in property rights of the firm. Block's proposal, which he dubs "capitalism without class power," calls for sharply increasing competition in capital markets and changing the governance structure of firms and banks. He traces much of the economic power of a very small class of wealth holders in the United States to the noncompetitive practices of big banks: more precisely, to strategic strikes of capital. Block would pass legislation limiting large and sudden movements of capital across borders. He would also increase competition in the financial sector by creating a series of quasi-public banks, both commercial and investment. Finally, he would, through legislation, change the composition of the boards of directors of firms, to consist of, for example, 35 percent employees, 35 percent asset holders, and 30 percent others, perhaps representing consumers or local citizens. (Recall Simon's social-republican property, in §2.) There would, however, be no limitations on private investment or on the stock market.

Block believes that these institutional changes would break the power of the wealthy on the economy and on politics, permitting the gradual equalization of incomes and wealth through an increasingly progressive tax policy. The main advantage of his proposal over the market-socialist proposals is that, he believes, his changes in the financial-corporate nexus would improve the efficiency and monitoring of firms; it is more doubtful such improvement would be possible under market socialism, where there is a much more radical break with traditional capitalist ownership. The main weakness of the proposal is that, at least on the surface, it does less to break the power of the wealthy on the economy than do the market-socialist proposals.

Cohen and Rogers advocate a system of "associative democracy." There are, they note, myriad organizations and associations of citizens of various kinds in modern capitalism; the Left has traditionally concentrated on only one kind of association, the trade union. Cohen and Rogers propose politically empowering all these associations. Thus, although *de jure* property rights in corporations might not change, *de facto* rights would, as active environmental associations and consumer associations, as well as unions, would force corporations to change their behavior. The economic model implicit behind the Cohen-Rogers view of advanced capitalism is a bargaining model, rather than a competitive one: the actions of firms and the wage structure, for example, are set more by bargaining than by markets, and Cohen and Rogers propose to change the relative bargaining power of the combatants. They view "factionalism" as a possible problem in their proposal, that society would become partitioned into groups each concerned only with its own parochial interest. But this may be a generic problem of all democracies.

One could levy a charge against this proposal that it is not achievable: who would organize the empowerment, which would obviously have to be from below, of this dense set of associations? Of course, this charge can also be levied against the other proposals: none of them is specific with respect to the process of transition from here to there, and it is therefore perhaps not fair to raise the issue especially for Cohen and Rogers. Nevertheless, if one were advising an Eastern European country that was trying to figure out what to do with its formerly state-owned firms, any of the first six proposals could be on the agenda, while the Cohen-Rogers proposal could not be. It may, however, be accurate to say that the Cohen-Rogers proposal is most immediately useful as a proposal for transition to a more democratic economy in advanced capitalist societies; it does, after all, further articulate the history of recent capitalism, in which political democracy has been one of the main conduits through which reform has taken place.

Let me reiterate that these seven proposals all assume that, in their economic behavior, people will go on acting much as they do under capitalism. The proposed institutions are putatively designed so that, given what we know of human behavior, the outcomes of the new economies (in particular, the distribution of income and power) would be different from those we observe in advanced capitalism. Furthermore, all the proposals are eclectic in the sense of using many of the microeconomic devices invented by capitalism: not only capital markets, but ways of monitoring firms and, more generally, providing incentives. I view this development as marking a new maturity on the Left. Some will view it as a defeatist revisionism that discards the Left's most cherished principles.

Where does social democracy fall along this gamut? I think socialists should count themselves victorious, in the

short run, if they can design systems that bring about the
degree of income equality and level of public services that
exist in the Nordic social democracies. I have no principled
objection to social democracy as a strategy in the short run.
I think, however, that very special conditions are necessary
for its success, namely, a highly disciplined labor movement
and a relatively homogeneous work force. Social democracy
worked in Sweden as long as the national organization of
the unions, the LO, was able to discipline member unions to
abide by the nationally negotiated wage agreement. Without this discipline, capitalists had no incentive to bargain
with the LO. The LO's ability to maintain this discipline
began evaporating when white-collar workers came to join
unions in large numbers. Thus, perhaps surprisingly, as
union density increased in Sweden in the 1970s and 1980s,
the LO became less powerful, leading to the demise of national negotiations. As Karl Moene and Michael Wallerstein (1993) write, when the unions became as diverse as
society itself, then it became difficult to maintain a united
front in national bargaining, which was the key to the social-
democratic compact. I therefore think that the social-
democratic model may have limited applicability in the
world.

§7

Public bads and the distribution of profits

One might object that organizing a market-socialist system that leaves the control of firms in the hands of profit-maximizing managers, as some of the proposals I described in §6 entailed, will not change much. The distribution of profits would be essentially equalized, but profits account for only ten to thirty percent of national income. And under market socialism profits may account for even less, because some revenue that takes the form of corporate profits in a capitalist system would instead take the form of interest payments to banks and their depositors. (See the Appendix for a computation of the profits that would accrue under the coupon system to an average householder in the United States.) I believe, however, that the partial equalization of income that would take place in these systems is only part of the story.

Classical arguments against capitalism discuss not only its bad distributional properties but its generation of what in modern economic parlance are called public bads. A public bad is a feature of a society from which everyone suffers. Public bads are often created by free-rider problems: it may be in the interest of each individual to perform a certain action on the assumption that everyone else will perform the same action; the collective result is a situation that is worse for everyone than if everyone had abstained from the action. A classic example of the free-rider problem producing a public bad is unemployment: it may be in the interest of each individual capitalist to lay off workers, but the collective effect when *many* employers take this step can be to induce a depression in which all capitalists and workers suffer.

There is an important class of public bads that increase the profits accruing to firms. Pollution is the prototypical example: it is a joint product of many firms and has a negative effect on people's welfare. Other examples are wars that increase profits, by lowering the price of imported inputs used by firms; noxious advertising, by cigarette companies; investment in firms doing business in South Africa;[1] and fast assembly-line speeds, or, more generally, the lack of enforcement of labor legislation, including legislation applying to occupational safety and health. All these practices increase profits—and often wages, as well—yet they also reduce the welfare of the population.

It has also been argued that a highly unequal distribution of wealth is itself a public bad, as it creates a kind of society that decreases the welfare of all—most obviously through the crime that it generates, less obviously through the lack of community that it engenders. Thus, low taxes on profits (which increase profits and do not mollify the effects of an unequal income distribution) are also a public bad in this sense.

Now any economy must admit some level of public bads. If we allowed no pollution, we would have no production; there are even some inefficiencies associated with full employment. There is, however, a socially optimal level of public bads, a level that best implements the trade-off for society as a whole between consumption of the public bad and consumption of output.[2] The problem in a capitalist economy is that there is a very small class of wealthy people who receive huge amounts of income as their share of firms' profits, and it is generally in the interest of these people to have high levels of the profit-increasing public bads. The positive effect from the public bad on the income of members of this class more than compensates them for the direct, negative effect on their welfare.[3] In this way, these public bads differ from the example of layoffs and unemployment, in which, hypothetically, even the capitalists suffered a net loss of welfare. People who stand to gain from them actively fight for, through political activity, high levels of profit-inducing public bads. The virtue of the market-socialist proposals is that there would exist no small, powerful class of people deriving gargantuan amounts of income from profits, hence no class would have such an interest in fighting for large levels of public bads. (I have included in the endnotes a concise model showing that the larger a person's ownership share of the means of production, the larger is that person's optimal level of profit-increasing public bads.)[4]

Consider the example of pollution. The citizens of industrialized countries have responded to industrial pollution by demanding legislation from their governments that limits the amount of pollution firms may create. It costs money to obey these laws, so compliant firms will generate lower profits. The loss of some profit is seen by most people to be balanced by the public good of a cleaner environment, but "most people" do not own the firms whose profits have been reduced. Those owners may prefer to have the private benefit of greater profits rather than the public good of fresh air or pure water. Large shareholders would therefore try to influence the political process—if that is the process that prescribes the level of pollution—to legislate allowances for higher permitted levels of pollution by the firm. This argument is only suggestive, however, for environmental regulation lowers the wage of the average citizen, as well. The example provided in note 4 checks the outcome when both the profit and wage effects are taken into account.

Or consider the public bad of supporting a regime of apartheid in South Africa by investing in companies that have subsidiaries there. Such investment, if it is undertaken, presumably increases profits, and perhaps wages, over alternative investments. From the argument given here, one would expect investment in apartheid to be more strongly supported by large shareholders. There is some evidence for this conjecture. The Public Employment Retirement System (PERS) in California, which represents many small investors (workers in state government jobs) and is the largest institutional investor in the U.S. stock market, recently divested itself of all stock in companies with South African subsidiaries. This divestment reportedly decreased the value of PERS's assets by 1 percent, a decrease which, evidently, the small investors represented by PERS were willing to sustain in order not to benefit from apartheid.[5] On the other hand, when have the boards of directors of corporations, representing on the whole their large shareholders, voluntarily decided not to invest in South Africa?

I do not make the blanket statement that if no class exists that derives huge amounts of income from corporate profits, then low levels of public bads will be forthcoming. But there is reason to believe, by the argument I've made above, that the redistribution of profit income could well have significant effects on social welfare. These effects would include not only a better distribution of income but a reduction in the amount of profit-inducing public bads. One must examine carefully, through modeling, the general-equilibrium welfare effects of mechanisms that preclude the formation of such a class. I have done some preliminary work on this topic, which I summarize next.[6]

§8

A model of a market-socialist economy

I will now be more specific about how market socialism might work. The model I shall describe in this section is not intended to be a complete description of a market-socialist economy. A number of matters are ignored, such as investment planning by the state, which is discussed in §§11 and 12. The purpose of the present model is to analyze one question only, the difference in the level of welfare of citizens that would come about as a consequence of different ways of defining property rights in firms when public bads are an issue.

I shall describe an economic environment upon which two possible politico-economic mechanisms shall be alternatively imposed, one capitalist, the other market-socialist. (This section is based on Roemer, 1992b.) The problem is to study the welfare of the population at the equilibrium induced by each mechanism. The environment is described as follows. There is only one good produced, which all people like to consume. There is also a public bad, think of it as pollution, which, given the available technology, is produced jointly with the good. One may think of this public bad as an input in each firm's production function, even if, in actuality, it is a joint product of the firm's production process, for the level of the public bad that the firm is allowed to "emit" indeed in part determines its production—the higher the permissible level of pollution, the greater the firm's production at a given level of the other input. That other input is the good itself. Thus firms produce a good using "inputs" of pollution and the good.

There are many citizens, of whom a small percentage are initially rich and a large percentage are initially not rich—call them poor. This means that, initially, the rich own a large amount of the good and the poor own a smaller amount. All citizens have the same preferences for consumption of the good, over time, and for the public bad: utility, a measure of a consumer's satisfaction, is increasing in consumption of the good and decreasing in consumption of the bad. The bad is public because all citizens must consume the same amount of it, namely, the amount of pollution "emitted" by firms. There are a number of firms in the economy. There is also a bank, which accepts deposits and makes loans.

There are three relevant dates at which things happen in the economy, call them dates 0, 1, and 2. Consumption of the good occurs at dates 0 and 2, and production and consumption of the public bad occur at date 2. Thus, a person's level of welfare, or utility, depends on consumption of the good and the bad at these two dates. In an economic model mathematical functions are used to express the relation between one measurement (such as utility) and one or more others (here consumption); often, however, the mathematical function is unknown or not required for the purpose of a particular discussion (which is the case here) and just the notation for the function is used. What is important to understand in this model is that the utility function u, the measure of a person's welfare, depends on consumption as defined above. Specifically, a person's utility function has the form $u(x_0, x_2, z)$, where x_0 is consumption of the good at date 0, x_2 is consumption at date 2, and z is consumption of the public bad at date 2.

There is uncertainty in the economy, which takes the following form. There are various possible *states of the world* that may occur at date 2. These states are brought about by events that should be thought of as occurring outside the model. What is relevant for us is that the production function of each firm—the relationship between the inputs used to produce the good and the quantity of the good produced—depends upon the state of the world. For example, the state of the world might be the weather, and the weather might affect the production of firms, which in this case are farms.

At date 0, all citizens are supposed to know the probabilities with which the various states will occur at date 2. At date 0, furthermore, each citizen owns, in addition to some amount of the good which characterizes her as rich or poor, an equal per-capita share of every firm in the economy. Each citizen must, at date 0, make consumption and investment decisions (how much of their shares of firms and their stock of the good should be consumed, how much invested for the future); the precise nature of these decisions depends upon the economic mechanism that shall be imposed. At date 1, citizens vote to determine the level of the public bad that will be permitted (in our example, the pollution that firms shall be allowed to emit). At date 2, one of the states of the world occurs, following which production takes place, with each firm emitting the amount of pollution that has been determined by vote at date 1. Output of the firms is distributed to citizens and consumed by them, according to the investment decisions they made at date 0. (See Figure 1.)

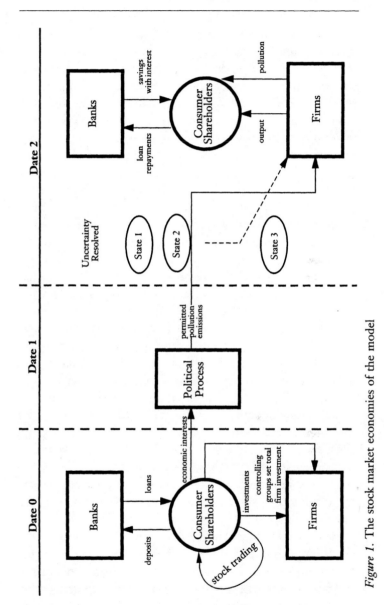

Figure 1. The stock market economies of the model

Let us now impose a capitalist financing mechanism on this economic environment—specifically, a stock market—that operates at date 0. People initially each own equal shares of all firms, but they can now trade these shares, the prices of the shares being denominated in units of the good. Thus, at date 0, a person can purchase a portfolio of stock, using her endowment of stock and her endowment of the good in trade. She also chooses how much of her endowment to consume at date 0 and how much to put in the bank at the going interest rate. (She may, alternatively, borrow from the bank.) For all stocks she acquires, she also must contribute to the firm a share of its total investment (which is its input of the good) equal to the share of its stock she has purchased.

After elections take place and the amount of the public bad is determined at date 1, and after the state of the world is revealed and production takes place at date 2, the citizen receives a share of output from each firm equal to the share of its stock she has purchased; she also receives her principal plus interest from the deposit she made in the bank at date 0 (or, alternatively, pays principal plus interest on the loan she took). Thus if, at date 0, citizens can predict the outcome of the vote at date 1, and if they know the prices for the stock of each firm and the interest rate, then they can choose a portfolio and consumption plan that maximizes their expected utility—that is, a plan that will lead on average to the best outcome for them. Every poor person will make the same optimal choice, and every rich person will make another optimal choice.

How does a firm choose its level of investment, the amount of input it shall use in production at date 2? At the equilibrium level of investment for each firm, citizens will purchase its stock in varying amounts. For each firm, either the rich or the poor will end up owning more than 50 percent of the stock. Call the group that ends up with more than half the stock the firm's controlling group. Then the firm's investment choice must be that which is optimal for its controlling group: that is, there can be no other investment choice that would have enabled its controlling shareholder type to have a higher expected utility.[1]

Finally, we must stipulate how people vote at date 1 on the permitted level of the public bad. Given the investment and consumption choices that people have made at date 0, each citizen has some optimal level for the amount of the public bad. (In this economy with just two types, there is one optimal level of the public bad for the poor and one for the rich.) Recall that increasing the amount of the public bad increases the output firms can produce at date 2, given their investment choices, and so each citizen has to consider a trade-off: increasing the permitted level of pollution will increase the consumption of the good of each citizen at date 2 but, on the other hand, it also decreases utility directly for each citizen (in the sense that for everyone the "quality of life" is lower). There is, in general, for each citizen type, a level of the public bad that optimizes this trade-off.

A classic and overly simple theory of voting would stipulate that the outcome of the election will be the level of the public bad preferred by the median voter or, in this case, preferred by the poor, who are in the majority. But this is unrealistic. I shall assume that the political process is sufficiently complex that both the rich and the poor have some impact on the determination of the level of the public bad. As a short cut to providing a full-fledged theory of this process, I shall simply stipulate that the outcome of the election maximizes some weighted average of the utilities of the poor and the rich, and I fix the weights used in this average as a characteristic of the political process.[2]

We are now prepared to state the concept of *capitalist politico-economic equilibrium* (CPEE). A CPEE is a set of stock prices for each firm's stock and an interest rate at date 0, a portfolio and consumption choice for each citizen at date 0, an amount of investment for each firm, and an amount of the public bad, such that:

(1) at that level of the public bad, at those prices and interest rate, and given the investment choice of each firm, the consumption and portfolio choice of each citizen at date 0 maximizes her expected utility;

(2) given the portfolio choices of each citizen, there is a controlling group for each firm, and the investment choice of the firm maximizes the expected utility for its controlling group, over all possible investment choices, given as well the level of the public bad;

(3) the level of the public bad is the outcome of the political process at date 1 (that is, it maximizes the appropriate weighted average of the utilities of the rich and the poor, given the portfolio choices of each individual);

(4) total bank deposits made and total bank loans extended are equal at date 0, and the demand and supply for the stock of each firm are equal.

Under suitable restrictions on the preferences of agents and the production functions of firms, a CPEE exists, and we can calculate it for specific choices of those functions.

Next, I describe a particular market-socialist politico-economic mechanism. It is the same as the capitalist mechanism but for one feature: one cannot purchase stock with the good but only with coupons. Each citizen begins with an endowment of the good, as before, and, say, 1,000 coupons, printed by the government. The prices of the firms' stocks are announced in coupons only. It is illegal to trade coupons for the good; one can only purchase stock of a firm with coupons, and stock can only be sold for coupons. Thus, each consumer has two budget constraints, one in terms of the good and one in terms of coupons. The coupon budget constraint states that a person cannot purchase shares valued in excess of 1,000 coupons. The good budget constraint states that total consumption at date 0 plus deposits at date 0 plus the amount of the good dedicated to the investment of firms in one's chosen portfolio cannot exceed one's initial endowment of the good.

All else is the same as in the description of the CPEE. We can now define a *market-socialist politico-economic equilibrium* (MSPEE) as consisting of a set of stock prices for each firm's stock, denominated now in coupons, and an interest rate at date 0, a portfolio and consumption choice for each citizen at date 0, an amount of investment for each firm, and an amount of the public bad, such that:

(1) at that level of the public bad, at those prices of stock and interest rate, and given the investment choice of each firm, the consumption and portfolio choice of each citizen at date 0 maximizes her expected utility;

(2) given the portfolio choices of each citizen, there is a controlling group for each firm, and the investment choice of the firm maximizes the expected utility for its controlling group, over all possible investment choices, given as well the level of the public bad;

(3) the level of the public bad is the outcome of the political process at date 1 (that is, it maximizes the appropriate weighted average of the utilities of the rich and the poor, given the portfolio choices of each individual);

(4) total bank deposits made and total bank loans extended are equal at date 0.

The wording here is exactly the same as in the definition of the CPEE, except that prices of stock are now denominated in coupons, not in units of the good. Under suitable conditions on preferences and production functions, an MSPEE exists, and, for specific choices of those functions, it can be calculated.

Thus one can, in principle, calculate the expected utilities of the rich and the poor in the equilibria that would be reached under the two politico-economic mechanisms. I shall report some of those calculations in a moment. But first let me conjecture, qualitatively, some of the differences that one might expect in politico-economic choices under the two mechanisms. What one should expect to happen in the capitalist economy is that the poor will sell a good deal of their initial endowment of firm shares to the rich, who shall pay for them with the good, which the poor shall consume at date 0. This will concentrate the ownership of stock in the hands of the rich, with two effects: the rich will be the controlling group in most firms, and hence the firms' investment choices will be in their interest; and the rich will have a greater interest than the poor in permitting a high level of the public bad, since they own such large fractions of the stock of firms (recall the discussion above, in §7).

In the coupon economy, however, the rich are precluded from buying controlling shares of all firms—for shares can only be purchased with coupons, and all citizens have the same initial endowment of coupons. One should expect, then, that at equilibrium the poor will be the controlling group in most firms, as they own the majority of coupons in society. Thus, the firms will choose their levels of investments in the interest of the poor. Furthermore, the rich will derive only a fairly small fraction of the consumption they will enjoy at date 2 from the profits of firm, and will not, therefore, desire as high a level of the public bad as they did in the capitalist economy.

All this is conjecture, for the general-equilibrium effects can be complicated. The only way to be sure what welfare will be in equilibrium is to prove a theorem or to make some calculations. I have no general theorems at this time, but I report the results of some calculations in Table 1.

Table 1 presents results from calculating the politico-economic equilibria under the capitalist system and the coupon system for this economic environment.[3] Equilibria were calculated for values of λ running between 0 and 1, where λ and $(1 - \lambda)$ are the weights assigned to the utility of the rich and the utility of the poor, respectively, in the determination of the political outcome, the level of the public bad. (Thus, for example, if $\lambda = 0.5$, then the utility of the rich and the poor are equally weighted in the political process that determines the level of the public bad.) Four aspects of the equilibria are reported: the level of the public bad ($\bar{z}$), the expected utilities of the poor (u^P) and of the rich (u^R), and total welfare, W, the sum of utilities in society.

Let us examine the results for the capitalist economy first. "Median-voter" politics occurs when $\lambda = 0$ (that is, the level of the public bad is the optimal level for the poor voters). As the influence of the rich (λ) increases in the elections, the level of the public bad at equilibrium rises. Intuitively, this occurs because, at all equilibria reported here, the rich end up purchasing a little over 50 percent of the stock of both firms. It turns out that the bank is not used at all, and so the income of the rich (and poor) at date 1 comes entirely from firm revenues. The rich want a higher level of the public bad than the poor because they own a substantial fraction of the firms: each rich person gets a little over 10 percent of each firm's revenue, while each poor person receives about one-half of one percent of each firm's revenue. Thus,

Table 1. General-equilibrium effects in coupon vs. capitalist economies

	Coupon equilibrium				Capitalist equilibrium			
λ	$\bar{z}$	u^P	u^R	W	$\bar{z}$	u^P	u^R	W
0.00	.884	2.46	11.51	291.10	.390	2.44	11.99	292.01
.04	.853	2.46	11.50	291.56	.463	2.45	12.09	292.79
.08	.822	2.47	11.49	291.99	.539	2.44	12.18	293.04
.12	.792	2.47	11.47	292.39	.616	2.44	12.25	292.86
.16	.762	2.48	11.46	292.74	.695	2.43	12.31	292.32
.20	.731	2.48	11.45	293.06	.775	2.42	12.37	291.46
.24	.702	2.49	11.43	293.33	.857	2.40	12.42	290.32
.28	.672	2.49	11.42	293.56	.941	2.39	12.46	288.95
.32	.643	2.49	11.40	293.75	1.03	2.37	12.50	287.36
.36	.614	2.49	11.39	293.89	1.11	2.35	12.54	285.57
.40	.585	2.50	11.37	293.97	1.20	2.32	12.56	283.61
.44	.556	2.50	11.35	294.01	1.29	2.30	12.59	281.49
.48	.528	2.50	11.33	293.98	1.37	2.28	12.61	279.21
.52	.500	2.50	11.31	293.90	1.47	2.25	12.63	276.80
.52	.473	2.50	11.28	293.75	1.56	2.22	12.65	274.26
.60	.445	2.50	11.26	293.53	1.65	2.19	12.66	271.60
.64	.418	2.50	11.23	293.23	1.74	2.16	12.67	268.82
.68	.392	2.49	11.21	292.86	1.84	2.13	12.68	265.94
.72	.366	2.49	11.18	292.40	1.93	2.10	12.69	262.96
.76	.340	2.49	11.15	291.84	2.03	2.07	12.69	259.88
.80	.314	2.48	11.11	291.18	2.12	2.03	12.69	256.71
.84	.289	2.47	11.08	290.41	2.22	2.00	12.69	253.46

Table 1. General-equilibrium effects in coupon vs. capitalist economies *(continued)*

	Coupon equilibrium				Capitalist equilibrium			
λ	$\bar{z}$	u^P	u^R	W	$\bar{z}$	u^P	u^R	W
.88	.265	2.47	11.04	289.51	2.32	1.96	12.69	250.12
.92	.241	2.46	11.00	288.47	2.42	1.93	12.69	246.70
.96	.217	2.45	10.95	287.26	2.52	1.89	12.69	243.21
1.00	.194	2.44	10.90	285.88	2.62	1.86	12.68	239.65

Note: u^P = utility of the poor; u^R = utility of the rich; W = total utility in the population.

increasing the level of the public bad makes a much bigger difference in date-2 revenue for the rich than for the poor, while they both suffer the same direct disutility from the public bad.

Generally speaking, as the rich's influence in the elections increases, the utility of the poor falls and the utility of the rich rises. This statement is not exactly true, however—for very small positive values of λ, the utility of the poor rises with λ, and for λ close to 1, the utility of both agents falls with increases in λ. (These apparent anomalies will be explained presently, when I discuss the results in the coupon economy.) If one thinks that total welfare is a significant welfare statistic (and one needn't, because utility functions are not necessarily endowed with any interpersonally comparable meaning), then total welfare reaches a maximum at around $\lambda = 0.08$.

Now, examine the results for the coupon economy. Notice, first, that as the rich gain more influence in the elections, the level of the public bad *falls*, the rich become *worse* off and the poor become *better* off (at least up to a point, around $\lambda = 0.5$). Indeed, the level of the public bad is lower in the coupon economy than in the capitalist economy for all $\lambda \geq 0.20$, and the difference is substantial: for example, at $\lambda = 0.55$, the level of the public bad in the coupon economy is about one-third its level in the capitalist economy. Total welfare is greater in the coupon economy for all $\lambda \geq .16$, and the poor (the vast majority of the population, in this environment) are better off in the coupon economy for all values of λ.

Here's the intuition for why the poor become better off as the political influence of the rich (λ) rises (up to about 0.5), an apparently paradoxical phenomenon. It turns out that substantial use of the bank occurs in the coupon economy: the poor borrow and the rich lend at date 0. The rich, who cannot purchase large shares of the firms from the poor on the coupon stock market, end up holding small fractions of both firms. By far the greater part of their income at date 2 comes from revenue from their bank deposits. The rich have little interest in increasing the value of the public bad, because revenues from firms add very little to their income at date 2. The poor, however, depend on firm revenues to pay off their loans at date 2, and so they want higher levels of the public bad. Hence, if the rich gain more influence in the political process (an increased value of λ), the value of the public bad chosen at date 1 will decrease. But if it decreases, the poor demand to borrow less at date 0, *ceteris paribus*, since they will have less firm revenue at date 1 to pay back loans. This decreases the equilibrium interest rate, an effect that is good for the poor, who are debtors, and hence increases their utility, while the decrease in the public bad decreases their utility. The net effect of these two effects is not easy to predict, and we see that for values of λ less than 0.5, the positive effect on the poor outweighs the negative.[4]

In comparing the equilibria under the two politico-economic mechanisms, notice that the poor (who in this specification constitute 95 percent of the population) are better off in the market-socialist equilibrium than in the capitalist equilibrium regardless of the degree of influence the rich have in the elections. This is not a general theorem, but it happens to be true in this model.

To summarize, the market-socialist mechanism prevents the free-rider problem that afflicts the poor under capitalism. In the capitalist economy, it is individually optimal for each poor person to sell the great majority of her initial endowment of shares to the rich, which creates a class of rich people who control firms and whose income depends on profits. The rich come to control firms, and through their influence on the political process, a high level of the public bad ensues. Under market socialism, the poor are precluded from liquidating their shares. The poor therefore remain the dominant shareholders and, as well, the rich turn out to be a force for lowering the level of the public bad. The net effects of these changes are not easy to predict in theory, but we have seen that, at least in one example, the poor end up better off in the market-socialist regime.

The coupon economy is equivalent to the capitalist economy except for one missing market: one cannot trade coupons for the good. Ordinarily it is assumed that traders will suffer when a market is removed, but that is not universally the case, especially when externalities are prevalent, as they are here.

A final comment on these results is in order. One advantage of having a coupon stock market in real life would be to prevent the poor from selling their shares *prematurely* to the rich, something one fears might happen if, let us say, firms in a formerly Communist economy were denationalized by distributing shares to all citizens, after which a fully liberalized stock market were opened.[5] This cannot occur in the coupon economy, since liquidation cannot occur. More formally, this phenomenon could happen under the capitalist politico-economic mechanism if the poor had poorer information than the rich about the probabilities with which the various states of the world occur at date 2. It is important to mention that this does not happen in the model whose equilibria are reported in Table 1: there, all agents are equally knowledgeable and rational. So, in real life, one might expect that the gap between the utility of the poor under the two mechanisms would be even greater than it is in Table 1.[6]

§9

The efficiency of firms under market socialism

At the end of §5, I said that the issue for market socialism was whether a politico-economic mechanism could be created under which firms would behave competitively—in particular, a system in which they would innovate. As Hayek pointed out, and as Kornai later ramified Hayek's point with the theory of the soft budget constraint, when the state controls firms, firm managers are to a large extent absolved from responsibility with regard to errors in judgment; more generally, inefficient practices will not be weeded out as they are in a competitive market environment. The model of §8 does not address this issue at all. That model's purpose was to examine the welfare of consumers at the general equilibria reached under different sets of property relations, under the assumption that the firm manager was a perfect agent of the firm's controlling group. Indeed, technological innovation was not an issue.[1] The purpose of this section (which is based in part on Bardhan and Roemer, 1992) is to argue that it is possible to establish institutions that would force firms to behave competitively in the coupon economy of §8.

As briefly described in §6, firms in the coupon economy would be organized around a fairly small number of main banks, as in the Japanese *keiretsu*. A main bank would be primarily responsible for putting together loan consortia to finance the operations of the firms in its group; it would, correlatively, be responsible for monitoring these firms.[2] The coupon stock market serves two of the three functions of a capitalist stock market: the movement in the coupon price of a firm's stock is a signal to banks and citizens about how well the firm is expected to perform, and the market allows citizens to choose how to bear risk. It does not perform the third function, of raising capital, which is here provided by banks. If the coupon price of a firm's stock falls (or more often, before that happens), the main bank would investigate how well the firm is being managed. It has an incentive to monitor the firms in its group effectively because, by so doing, it keeps its firms profitable and thereby able to pay back their loans. Having profitable firms as clients gives the bank a good reputation, making it easier for it to continue to raise money to finance the operations of firms in its group.

But why should the bank, which is itself a publicly owned institution, perform its monitoring job well?[3] Who, that is, would monitor the monitors? The principal question is whether the banks would operate with sufficient independence of the state, making decisions about firms using economic and not political criteria. Bardhan and I do not believe that we have a definitive solution to this problem, although we view the following features of the economy as ones which would induce banks to do their job properly.

First, there should be constitutional provisions that grant the banks considerable independence from state control. This would, for example, include guarantees that bank management be evaluated on economic criteria only—that managers be hired on a managerial labor market, for instance, by a board of directors. How should the boards of directors of large state banks be chosen? One possibility is suggested by Robert Pollin (1993): they should be elected by citizens in the bank's district. Block (1992) has other proposals, referred to earlier, for democratizing the choice of bank directors. These proposals provide some (although not fool-proof) protection against the banks' directors becoming a ruling class who represent the wealthy.

Second, the concerns that the managers would have for their personal reputations should act as an antidote to sus-ceptibility to political pressure. In Japan, even though banks have been closely regulated by the Ministry of Finance, managers are keen to preserve their reputation as good monitors, and banks compete in seeking the position of main bank for well-run firms. The managerial labor market will not forget if a bank manager forgives bad loans or tolerates nonperforming firms too often.

Third, incentive features would be a part of the salary structure of bank management.

Fourth, the doors of international product competition must be kept open. Competition from abroad would act as a check on laxity of the institutional monitors.

Fifth, as Sah and Weitzman (1991) have suggested, there should be well-publicized precommitments by banks before large investment projects begin. These agreements would impose liquidation should the performance of firms at pre-specified dates not exceed prespecified levels. The public nature of these precommitments would preclude the soft-budget-constraint problems that Mathias Dewatripont and Eric Maskin (1993) have studied, as a result of which it is in the interest of public banks to renegotiate loans on poorly performing projects.

Sixth, some significant fraction of the shares of banks

should not be held by the government but by pension funds, insurance companies, and other institutions. These institutions would be interested in the banks' profitability and would act to counter political pressure from the state.

In sum, the banks' independence from political control would be enforced by a series of legal and economic measures; banks would constitute a hard layer of economic accountability between the state and the management of firms. Colin Mayer and his co-authors have argued, in several papers, that a system in which banks monitor firms is preferable to the takeover process as the mechanism guaranteeing firm performance in capitalist economies;[4] there seems ample reason to believe that a similar mechanism can be adapted to a market-socialist economy.

If banks monitor firms aggressively and firms must depend on banks for finance, and if the doors to international trade are open, firms will innovate. Under capitalism, innovations are designed in the R&D departments of large firms, or they enter the economy through the formation of new, small firms. All seven of the proposals discussed in §6 would permit the formation of small private firms. In Bardhan's and my managerial proposals, it is envisaged that many growing firms would eventually be bought by large firms in the "public" sector, as happens under capitalism. Or, the government might auction the private firm to firms in the public (coupon) sector, the proceeds going to the erstwhile owner. Perhaps joining the public sector would be a prerequisite to receiving loans from the main banks or loans at preferential interest rates. There would be a statute requiring nationalization of private firms that reach a given size—a size at which their erstwhile owners would become wealthy from the state's purchase of their firm. Allowing a private sector under these conditions should provide almost the same incentives that exist in capitalism for those who form new firms in order to bring innovations to market. Nationalizing firms at a certain level would prevent the emergence of a class of capitalists capable of influencing politics and economic policy by virtue of their economic control of significant sectors of the means of production.

It should be noted that there is vigorous disagreement among finance economists concerning the relative efficacy of banks versus the stock market/takeover process as monitoring institutions. The coupon economy I have proposed combines both institutions: the coupon price of stock indicates to banks how well investors think firms are doing and gives them at least two reasons to intervene in poorly performing firms: first, to preserve their reputations, and second, in those cases where banks hold positions in the firm to protect their own investments. (In the Bardhan model, banks own shares of firms in their *keiretsu*, and so this second mechanism works as well.)

What are the contentious points in the monitoring (bank versus stock market) debate? The stock market, viewed as a market for corporate control, essentially puts firms continually on auction. As Franks and Mayer (1992) point out, auctions are efficient only if there are good credit markets, so that those with good managerial ideas can borrow and bid for firms. We lack perfect credit markets, indeed, in large part because creditors cannot costlessly inspect how reliable the would-be borrower is. If, as well, investors are myopic (a point on which there is disagreement), then stock prices will fall when firms take actions that are optimal in the long run but that engender short-run decreases in profits and dividends. For these reasons, the perpetual auction system in which the stock market consists may be an inefficient mechanism for monitoring firm management. Stiglitz (1985) also presents several reasons that the takeover process via the stock market may be inefficient. For instance, if shareholders of Firm A are rational, and if it is true that Firm B, which is tendering a takeover offer for Firm A, would in fact increase Firm A's value under reorganization, then shareholders of Firm A should not sell their shares but should hold them and share in the capital gain. Therefore, the takeover will not occur.

As Franks and Mayer (1990) discuss, in Germany and Japan monitoring is done by a committee system, where the committee consists of people knowledgeable about the industry. Lacking perfect capital markets, this system may well be superior to the stock market.

Douglas Diamond (1991) argues that a bank monitoring system can be more efficient than a stock market when investors have imperfect information about firms and their managements. If a firm has no reputation (it is young) or a poor reputation, bank monitoring signals to investors and bondholders that the firm will be well run, thus lowering the cost of capital to the firm. But bank monitoring involves its own costs to the firm: the bank must learn about the firm and monitor it, and the firm will pay for this in the interest the bank charges on its loans to the firm. (A bank should be financially involved in the firms it monitors, for this signals to investors that the bank has an interest in monitoring the firm carefully.) Firms that have good reputations, however, need not use bank monitoring: they can go directly to investors without intermediation and save the monitoring costs. Investors know they will self-monitor to preserve their good reputations. Thus, according to Diamond, some firms should use bank monitors and others should not.

Michael Porter (1992), in an article summarizing the results of a large study conducted by the Harvard Business School, presents a more negative view of the stock market than I have thus far taken. He writes that in the United States, in contrast to Germany and Japan, the investment policy of firm management is driven by the necessity of maintaining high stock prices. Because many stock-market investors, in particular institutional ones, are driven by a search for short-term capital gains, investment policy becomes myopic. The stock market, in a word, is grossly inefficient. In Germany and Japan, the main owners of firms, which are institutional, regard themselves as permanent owners and do not trade stock; stock prices are determined, as in the United States, by investors with short-term horizons, but stock prices do not determine firms' investment policies. The institutional owners of firms will not fire firm management if it pursues a long-run investment policy that leads in the short run to low stock prices. Porter concludes that the Japanese and German systems of management by committee, to use the phrase of Franks and Mayer, leads to a long-term orientation in investment policy, which is much closer to being socially optimal than the investment policy induced by the U.S. stock market. The article ends by recommending a number of reforms in the U.S. capital-allocation system that would effectively shelter firm management from the vagaries of the stock market, induced by the behavior of myopic investors.

Thus, expert opinion on the ability of the stock market to allocate capital efficiently and monitor firms well varies greatly. (I have not bothered to elaborate more fully here the often-cited view, with which readers are probably familiar, that holds that the stock market is the key to the efficiency of a capitalist economy.) The coupon economy I have described combines stock markets with institutional monitoring through banks: one could design the system to permit varying degrees of influence that the stock market could have on capital allocation and firm monitoring, depending on one's view concerning the efficiency of the stock market. My own view is strongly influenced by the evidence cited in the Porter article, and so I would recommend safeguards that enabled banks to monitor firms independently of what the stock market was saying. (This is not to say the informational function of the stock market is useless.) Publicly constituted boards of directors would be one such safeguard.

Finally, how would the market-socialist economy deal with international capital flows? This would be a question for the electorate, but I see no reason to forbid foreign investment in the domestic public sector. The degree of foreign investment and the associated rights of foreign investors can be circumscribed by law. Foreign investors would not have coupons, of course, but would invest real capital in return for some share of profits. This would implicitly set up a valuation of coupons in terms of currency, and the possibility arises that citizens might use foreign firms as their agents to invest their capital in domestic firms. This would have to be outlawed, and I believe that such a law could be enforced quite effectively—at least in countries at fairly high levels of development.

Would domestic firms attempt to set up foreign subsidiaries to escape high wages at home? The extent to which this would be allowed would be controlled by law. This is an important sense in which the firms of the market-socialist economy would remain socially controlled: they would not necessarily have the right freely to export capital.

Circumscribing this right would go a long way to changing the bargaining relationship between capital and labor. On the face of it, this prohibition would seem to be a pitfall for workers: even though they would more easily be able to win high wages, it is also possible that, if capital lacked the option to move abroad, domestic goods might be priced out of the international market, leading to unemployment and recession. But one must note that the incentives of workers would not be the same in the market-socialist economy as they are in the capitalist economy: each worker would be receiving, on average, her per-capita share of total profits from the public-sector firms as well as her wage, and her interest would be in maximizing her total income. Roughly speaking, each worker would be interested in maximizing *national income*, not the national wage bill, for she would receive a per-capita share of national income. (This is only "roughly speaking," for not all workers would receive the same wage, and there would also be a private sector that contributed to national income.) In particular, if all workers were identical in skills and there were no private sector, then the optimal wage for the worker would be the competitive (i.e., Walrasian) wage for the economy where each owns a per-capita share of all firms: for this wage engenders full employment and maximizes national income. Thus, if we assume that labor unions coordinated their activities through a national association, then wage demands would not be excessive in the market-socialist economy, in the sense of bringing about unemployment and low national income.

Finally, I must emphasize that I envisage the coupon economy as a desirable model of market socialism only when the economy can support sophisticated financial institutions and regulation. (For economies at low levels of development, the Bardhan *keiretsu* model is, I believe, superior.) Without a monitoring organ like the Securities and Exchange Commission in the United States, it would be difficult to control black-market transactions in which wealthy citizens purchased coupons from poor citizens with cash. (With an organization like the S.E.C., the government can account for all exchanges on the stock market. All exchanges of stock would be implemented by computer and would be made at market, or coupon, prices. In particular, it would not be possible to give stock away, or to sell it to one's child, for example, at a below-market price.) There are other ways that firms could accommodate investors who wished to capitalize their coupon portfolio: some firms could become "cash cows," selling off their capital stock and paying the proceeds out to shareholders as dividends. The coupon price of the shares would eventually fall to zero, but by that time the shareholders would have effectively capitalized their coupon holdings. Cash cows must be prevented by regulation—for example, by limiting dividend payouts not to exceed earnings.

Cash cows and black-market sales of coupons (which would not, in any case, be possible with central computer accounting) can to some extent be prevented by the creation of financial instruments enabling those who need a large sum of cash (to start a small business, for example) to get it by using their coupon portfolios as collateral. Banks could lend the expected present value of a coupon portfolio to a citizen, taking over the portfolio and managing it during the period of the loan, and servicing the loan with income from the portfolio. If this kind of instrument were used on a large scale and banks came to control the coupon portfolios of a substantial fraction of the population, one would have to ask whether the decentralization of economic power, necessary for the decreased levels of public bads as described in §7, would be reversed. The answer may be that the banks should be publicly owned and have popularly chosen directors. The goal would be to design the governing structure of banks so that they would not attempt to influence the political process (for example, in the determination of the level of environmental protection) as if they were large, wealthy investors. (See Table 1 in §8.)

§10

The Yugoslav experiment

Yugoslavia was one of the two European countries in which the antifascist partisan movement, led by the Communists under Marshal Tito, was sufficiently strong and respected by the populace to take power at the end of the war (Albania was the other). There was, in this sense, a socialist revolution from below in Yugoslavia. In 1948, Stalin expelled Yugoslavia from the Cominform, and soon thereafter the country engaged in a massively new experiment. It abandoned Soviet-type central planning and organized production from below through a network of firms managed by workers. From 1949 to 1970, the Yugoslavian growth rate was among the highest in Europe, and this was attributed by many to the decentralization of economic activity and the use of markets.

By the beginning of the 1980s, however, crisis and stagnation had set in, with low or negative growth rates accompanied by high inflation. We must ask whether Yugoslavia was, indeed, a real experiment in market socialism and, if it was, whether its degeneration and collapse constitute proof of the failure of market socialism.

I am not concerned here with what happened in Yugo-slavia for the two decades following the war, for in that period Yugoslavia was a success story: so if it was, indeed, a market-socialist economy in those years, that part of its history would constitute no proof that market socialism is a chimera. The salient period begins sometime in the 1970s.

The following discussion is based mainly upon Lydall (1989). What emerges with utmost clarity is that the essential condition of what I have called the fifth generation of market-socialist models failed to hold in Yugoslavia: firms were not run on a competitive, profit-maximizing basis but were intensively interfered with by political authorities. Not only was competition between firms actively prevented, but the soft-budget-constraint syndrome was ubiquitous: firm managers could not be held responsible for losses, because investment decisions were often made by local political authorities. The state took responsibility for losses, covered them by printing money, and thereby unleashed inflation.

Although the central government was not intimately involved in firms, power devolved to local governments, which were. Federalism in Yugoslavia meant that each of the six republics tried to remain self-sufficient: there was, consequently, much inefficiency in the duplication of investment projects. Having a number of firms (in different republics) producing the same products might have led to competition, except that republics erected trade restrictions to protect their local enterprises. Capital mobility across republican borders was likewise discouraged.

The operations of firms were severely restricted. A firm had no incentive to open up a subsidiary, for the subsidiary would, by law, become an independent firm. Firms were often compelled to take on unemployed workers whom they did not need. One scholar estimated that 40 percent of workers in the "nonproductive" sector (services, banking, etc.) and 10 percent of the workers in the "productive" sector were unnecessary. These may have been gross underestimates. A Japanese team considering an investment in a Yugoslav firm said it would only take part if one-half the workers were laid off. A Yugoslav firm making electric motors, thought to be a well-operated firm, produced one-fourth the output of its Italian counterpart with four times the labor force. Firms were discouraged from competing with each other: there was no free entry, and it was unheard of for a firm to compete with another one in its own commune (district). Moreover, firms were protected from competition by imports, which were severely restricted.

Management was appointed by political authorities, although, in principle, it could be fired by an assembly of workers. (The workers' assemblies became known as rubber stamps for management proposals.) Managers received no training and were frequently innocent of knowledge of the industry in which they worked. Furthermore, their power was highly circumscribed: they could not, for example, lay off workers, nor could they introduce schemes to reward hard work and penalize shirking. They spent much of their time in meetings with political organizations: one researcher estimated that a Yugoslav manager spent 10 percent of his time in activities relevant to production and sales, activities on which a German manager would spend 90 percent of his time.

Because managers were unable to fire workers, there was high absenteeism and idleness on the job. Workers often carried out moonlighting activity on the job. It was estimated that the average working day in some sectors was only three-and-one-half hours; workers spent about 150 days a year on the job. Yugoslav workers who migrated to Germany contrasted the pace of work there with the pace at home.

These are only a few of many indications of how little the Yugoslav economy resembled the kind of market socialism that I have described in §§8 and 9. Most of the fatal features of the system originated in the control that local political authorities maintained over firms. Politicians curtailed competition, both from other national firms and from imports, and sharply circumscribed the prerogatives of management. Firm managers were appointed on political criteria, not on the basis of expertise; when their policies failed, large investments were underwritten by a government that paid creditors by printing money.

Finally, there was deep hostility toward the private sector. Employment in a private business was limited to five or ten employees. When private firms did begin, they were harassed by myriad permits, regulations, and arbitrary taxation.

Ben-Ner and Neuberger (1990) characterize Yugoslavia as having gone through six economic systems since 1947; the political struggle that determined this evolution was between centralizers, who desired more central planning and federal power, and decentralizers, who wanted each republic to control its own economy. The centralizers also represented the poorer regions of the country and advocated transfers to them from the richer regions; the decentralizers were generally from the richer regions. Ben-Ner and Neuberger characterize the system that came into existence in 1974, with a new constitution, as one of negotiated planning, in which republican governments were to coordinate investment plans of enterprises. The system did not work, in part because the legal machinery was not in place to enforce agreements, and because it was based on an assumption of cooperative behavior among enterprises for which there was no material basis. The central planning that existed under this system, they say, was less effective than "indicative planning" had been. (Indicative planning, principally undertaken in postwar France, refers to government coordination of plans for different sectors of an economy. Central planning of the Soviet type, in contrast, involved direct commands from government to firms about what to produce.)

At the most general level, the failure of the Yugoslav experiment was due to the unwillingness of those in control of the state organs, national and republican, to allow firms autonomy and to encourage competition. One cannot say that this was a necessary consequence of political dictatorship (by the League of Communists), for political dictatorship in the four Asian tigers has not precluded rapid economic development. Nor is planning itself the culprit, for there surely has been intensive planning in Singapore, Taiwan, and South Korea. The key differences between the two types of dictatorship lie in attitudes toward competition, toward the training of expert management, and toward the autonomy of the firm, along with an important corollary: hard budget constraints. As Hayek noted in 1935, if the political authorities control the investment and personnel decisions of the firm, they cannot simultaneously hold the management accountable for its losses.

§11

State intervention in the economy

Although I have thus far put the emphasis on the functioning of the market, there would also be state intervention in a market-socialist economy. Welfare-state measures would exist, in particular, to further equalize the real distribution of income.[1] Unemployment would continue to exist, because firms would make decisions independently and based on market criteria; these measures would therefore include unemployment benefits and retraining programs for workers. Much has been written on the welfare state, and I see no need to add to this literature here.[2]

In addition to undertaking social-welfare programs, I envision market socialism as engaging in investment planning, both by providing incentives for firms to invest in particular sectors or regions and by direct government investment. There are three main reasons for wanting to involve the state in investment planning:

(1) Because of positive externalities from investment. Examples are investment in research and development and in education. Both activities produce benefits for society or the economy as a whole that are not fully captured by the agents

who may finance them, and hence individual firms will not be induced to invest as much as they should, from the social viewpoint, in these activities. More generally, the skills of workers are upgraded by working on new technologies; this kind of education is perhaps more important for economic development than what takes place in schools. Therefore, investment by the state is appropriate.

(2) To create public goods. Investments of this type are exemplified by infrastructural projects: highways, airports, dams, railroads, and communication systems. These inputs are essential to the production of many firms; they are, in most cases, more efficiently provided by government than by private finance. Adam Przeworski (1992) suggests that the optimal rate of government investment in advanced economies is between 20 and 25 percent of total investment.

(3) To compensate for incomplete markets. Because futures markets in general are nonexistent—markets in which firms could insure themselves against the contingency that their investment will turn out to be unprofitable—the level of investment in a market economy is almost surely nonoptimal. A firm wants to maintain "flexibility," which means it may decide not to invest until some uncertainty is resolved in a future period. Maintaining flexibility, in this sense, may be socially optimal, but in general it is not. Joaquim Silvestre and I (1992) have studied a model with three periods, in which a firm must invest in the period before production occurs. (The three-period structure captures the essential element that causes investment to be often inefficient in market economies, the fact that it takes time in an uncertain world.) During the second period, either a good or a bad shock will occur in the economy—say, the firm's international orders will either be large or small. Firms can only invest once. Thus, a firm can choose to invest in period 1, enabling it to produce in periods 2 and 3—but then it must

choose its investment level (which determines its future production function) before the nature of the shock is revealed. Alternatively, it can wait until the shock is revealed and invest in period 2—but then it can produce only in period 3, not in period 2. We show that, for a certain range of parameter values of the model, the firm will choose flexibility, that is, to wait until the shock has occurred, invest in period 2, and produce only in period 3. There is, however, a Pareto-superior allocation that can be achieved with government intervention. The government promises to subsidize, *ex post*, the firm's investment in period 1 should the period-2 shock turn out to be bad, paying for the subsidy by taxation. This induces the firm to invest in period 1, which results in an equilibrium outcome in which everyone (both firm owners and workers) are better off.

Why is this kind of insurance not provided by private markets in capitalist economies? Often, significant "moral hazard," the possibility that the insured will take fewer precautions against a bad outcome because he is insured, may be involved; the firm may be responsible, by virtue of its own negligence, for a "bad shock," such as a diminution in orders received in the second period. Presumably, the government should not insure firms in cases like these. But there are also bad shocks for which the firm is clearly *not* responsible, such as a recession of the economy in a future period. The government, in times of recession, might be able to increase investment (and hence employment) by paying off firms in the contingency that the growth rate does not exceed a given rate in a future period. The firm has no incentive to shirk with this kind of contract. This kind of investment insurance becomes riskier for the government the more open the economy; it would only be a wise move in cases of recession that are clearly induced by a domestic failure of investment, due to firms' pessimistic estimates concerning the future vitality of the economy.

But if such insurance is efficient and not subject to problems of moral hazard and adverse selection, why has it not been organized by private insurance markets? The answer is that the insurance would have to be mandatory for all firms (or large firms) in the economy. For the purpose of having the insurance is to create an environment in which all firms *would* invest in period 1, and hence the bad state (a low growth rate) would not materialize in period 2. Universal insurance would indeed vastly lower the probability that the bad state occurs—but clearly only *universal* insurance does this. Mandatory insurance cannot be organized without state intervention.[3]

Two types of economic planning must be distinguished: planning which is used in the case of market failure, and planning which is used to replace markets when they are not failing. Nineteenth-century Marxism included a general condemnation of markets; to this one may trace the intellectual origins of the pervasive planning of the Soviet-type economies. Once pervasive planning is begun, it creates a political constituency for its own continuation, namely, those planners and bureaucrats in whom economic power becomes vested. Indeed, both kinds of planning create such a constituency, which must be counted as a social cost: the difference between the two is that, in the first case, there is also a social benefit. The neoliberal claim that planning always is a net cost to society is naively based on the view that real market failures never occur because those affected by an apparent market failure can always voluntarily negotiate a Pareto-improvement. As Silvestre (1992) has convincingly argued, this belief is often justified by an illegitimate appeal to the so-called Coase theorem, which only holds in a world with zero transactions costs.[4] But we do not live in such a world.

It is fitting to conclude this section with a quotation from Przeworski (1992):

> [I]f a Martian were asked to pick the most efficient and humane economic systems on earth, it would certainly not choose the countries which rely most on markets. The United States is a stagnant economy in which real wages have been constant for more than a decade and the real income of the bottom 40 percent of the population declined. It is an inhumane society in which 11.5 percent of the population, some 32 million people, including 20 percent of all children, live in absolute poverty. It is the oldest democracy on earth but also one with the lowest voting rates among democracies and the highest per capita prison population in the world. The fastest developing countries in the world today are among those where the state pursues active industrial and trade policies; the few countries in the world in which almost no one is poor today are those in which the state has been engaged in massive social welfare and labor market policies.

§12

A digression on investment planning

Many observers think that *planning* must always mean *administrative allocation of resources*, as it did, in large part, in the Soviet-type economies. That view is incorrect, as we know from the examples of indicative planning in France, the Ministry of Trade and Industry (MITI) in Japan, and Scandinavian corporate-tax policy, among many others. In §11, I have given another example of planning, one that is accomplished by government-organized insurance rather than by direct government allocations of investment goods. In the present section, I describe studies undertaken with my co-authors Ignacio Ortuño and Joaquim Silvestre, in which we ask the question: What is the *scope* for investment planning in a socialist economy committed to the use of markets? And what are the *relative advantages of various instruments* that may be used to carry it out?[1] Then, by way of practical illustration, I review briefly the history of recent investment planning in Taiwan.

Let me frame the discussion by outlining a model of a prototypical economic environment. In describing this environment, I do not presuppose any economic mechanism,

95

capitalist or socialist, but simply lay out the temporal and physical nature of production and investment. Imagine a society that exists for two periods, with a population of citizens who work and consume in each period. There is one sector that produces the economy's single investment good (say, steel), and a number N of sectors that produce the different consumption goods. There are a number of firms in each sector; perhaps different firms in a single sector have different technologies. Citizens supply labor to firms and consume the consumption goods in each period: each shall try, under any economic mechanism, to choose an amount of consumption, and the timing of consumption, over the two periods that maximizes his particular utility, subject to whatever income (budget) constraint he faces.

During the first period, all firms must produce with whatever capital stock they have on hand, but they may place orders for the investment good during the first period, which will augment their capital stock in the second period. The volume of investment is most proximately determined by the division of society's labor in the first period between the production of consumption goods and the production of the investment good. The more investment good produced and invested, the greater will be the production capabilities of the economy in the second period, when only consumption goods are produced. Thus, a decision to invest more is a decision to trade off present consumption for future consumption.

Now impose a capitalist economic mechanism on this environment, one in which the firms are privately owned, there is some particular distribution of ownership of firms, and markets allocate resources. Each citizen owns the right to a certain fraction, perhaps zero, of the profits of each firm. (If this economy is anything like actual capitalist economies, there is a large class of people who hold almost no corporate stock: in the United States, the wealthiest 10 percent of households own 83 percent of all corporate stock.) We study the capitalist economy in a state of market equilibrium, also known as a *Walrasian equilibrium*, after the nineteenth-century economist Léon Walras.

A Walrasian equilibrium for this economy can be described briefly as follows. First, consider markets and prices. There is a price for each consumer good in each period, for the investment good in the first period (that's a total of $2N + 1$ prices so far), and for each kind of labor in each period. Say there are K kinds or qualities of labor, or types of skill, in the economy. In addition, there is an interest rate at which citizens can save or borrow and firms can borrow. Thus there are $2N + 2 + 2K$ prices in this economy. I shall assume that all citizens and firms know today's prices and either know or correctly forecast the prices of the second period.[2] Facing any set of these $2N + 2 + 2K$ prices, economic actors—firms and citizens—behave as follows:

(1) Each consumer-good firm demands amounts of the various kinds of labor and an amount of investment good and supplies amounts of its output in both periods so as to maximize its total discounted profits over the two periods at given prices. We assume that each firm is small relative to its market, so that it need not take into account the effect of its production on the price of output: it behaves as a price-taking competitor.

(2) The investment-good firm chooses an amount of the investment good to supply and an amount of each kind of labor to demand, to maximize its profits (in the first period), at given prices.

(3) Each citizen has a lifetime budget consisting of her wage income from supplying her labor endowment in

the two periods to firms plus her profit income from firms, derived from her ownership shares. Given this lifetime budget, she decides upon an amount to save or borrow in the first period and an amount of each consumer good to demand in both periods, to maximize her utility subject to her lifetime budget constraint. Savings in the first period are returned with interest in the second period.

(4) The timing of economic activity is as follows. At the end of each period, firms pay out the profits to shareholders and pay wages to workers. Every firm sells its output at the end of the period in which it is produced. Thus firms retain no earnings and must borrow to pay for the investment good, which they purchase at the end of period 1 but which is not counted as a cost of production until period 2.

Such is the behavior of every economic actor in this economy facing any combination, or vector, of $2N + 2 + 2K$ prices. A price vector is a *Walrasian price equilibrium* if:

(5) The total demand for each commodity and each kind of labor equals the total supply for each commodity and each kind of labor, and the total supply of savings equals the demand for investment. That is, all markets clear at these prices.

Under suitable conditions upon the nature of preferences or utilities of the citizens and on the nature of firms' technologies, a Walrasian price equilibrium will exist, given the ownership structure of firms and the endowments of labor possessed by citizens. If we assert that the normal state of a capitalist economy is to be at such an equilibrium, we can infer aspects of resource allocation in a capitalist economy from aspects of the resource allocation at a Walrasian equilibrium of the model.

In particular, there will be some particular *pattern of sectoral investment* at a Walrasian equilibrium. Total investment of firms will equal total savings of consumers. A consumer deciding how much to save is only trying to maximize his lifetime utility, given the prices of the consumer goods, the interest rate, and his budget (we assume that he correctly predicts the profits of each firm in which he has an interest, as his shares of these are part of his budget); each firm decides upon its investment only with an eye to maximizing the present value of profits, not with an eye to satisfying the demands of consumers.

Notice that the distribution of income will be unequal in this economy for two reasons: some citizens will be endowed with qualities of labor that are more valuable, at equilibrium wages, than those of others, and profits may be distributed in a highly unequal fashion. Note also that there are no taxes in this economy—in order to simplify the analysis, I have made the unrealistic assumption that there are no transfer payments or public goods of any kind for which taxes would be needed. We are examining a simple prototype of an economy where everyone is able-bodied, or can otherwise survive on his income, and all final goods are private goods.

I will now outline how a market-socialist mechanism could allocate resources in this same economic environment while addressing the unequal distribution of profits and the perhaps undesirable pattern of investment of the Walrasian equilibrium.[3] In this model there is a democratic process that elects a party that is empowered to implement its economic program. This program consists of two planks: a proposed distribution of the after-tax profits of all (public) firms among the citizens, and a proposed level and pattern of investment for the economy. Thus, in the socialist economy, the shares of firm profits going to citizens are chosen to be roughly equal. One mechanism for assuring this was described in §8, although the present model is simplified by the absence of a stock market: thus we shall simply assume that firms distribute profits net of corporate taxes to citizens in the politically determined way. There is a manager of each firm whose job it shall be to maximize profits of that firm, facing market prices. Each citizen's income shall consist of her wage income, from selling her labor power to firms in both periods, and her social dividend (that is, her share of total profits of public firms after taxes). In the particular mechanism—one possible variant of market socialism—that I now describe, there shall be taxes collected by the government only on the profits of firms.

The instruments that the government shall use to influence the pattern of investment are discounts and surcharges on the market interest rate. The central bank shall be empowered to lend money to firms, with a specific interest rate discount or surcharge for each consumer-good sector. A firm in a particular sector can borrow at its specific discount; citizens save or borrow at the market rate. I now define a *Lange equilibrium* for this economy, so named because Oskar Lange first proposed that interest rates be used by the socialist government to regulate investment. A Lange equilibrium is a set of prices for all goods in each period ($2N + 1$ prices), a set of wages in each period ($2K$), an interest rate, a set of discounts on the interest rate (N of these), and a set of tax rates on corporate profits (N of these, too), at which the following happens:

(1) Each consumer-good firm demands an amount of labor of each quality and an amount of the investment good, and each firm supplies an amount of its output

in both periods that maximizes the present value of profits over two periods. In particular, note that it will be relatively more profitable for firms receiving higher interest rate discounts to invest, since investment is financed by loans.

(2) Each investment-good firm demands labor and supplies its output in those amounts that maximize profits.

(3) Each citizen calculates her budget as the sum of her labor income and her social dividend (the share of after-tax corporate profits that she receives). She chooses the pattern of consumption over two periods, and the amount she saves or borrows, that maximizes her utility subject to her budget constraint.

(4) The central bank pays out interest to citizens in the second period at the market rate, and it collects interest from firms at various discounted rates. Even if savings equals investment, as it shall in equilibrium, the receipts and payments of the central bank will not balance because of the difference in interest rates. Taxes collected from corporate profits must exactly cover the central bank's deficit.

(5) The total supply of every good and each kind of labor equals the total demand for every good and each kind of labor, and the total supply of savings of citizens equals the total value of investment goods demanded by firms.

Figure 2 diagrams the exchange of money and goods in the economy.

We can prove that many Lange equilibria exist in this economy. Suppose the government wants to implement a particular sectoral pattern of investment in the economy. If this vector of investment levels lies in a certain well-defined

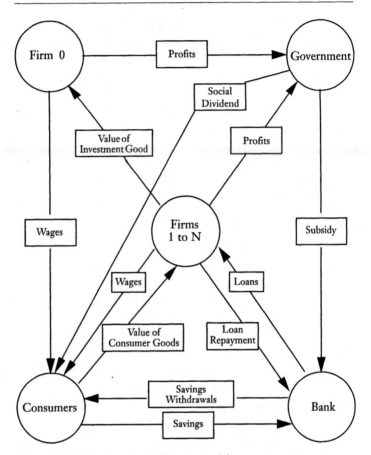

Figure 2. Money flows in the Lange model

set, then the government can announce interest rate discounts and corporate tax rates such that a Lange equilibrium will be reached at which the investment levels in
sectors are precisely the levels specified by that vector. Just
as one assumes that the market finds the Walrasian equilibrium in a capitalist economy, so we assume that the market will find, after the government's announcement, this

Lange equilibrium in the market-socialist economy. One assumption is as robust as the other.

Let me qualitatively describe how the government sets interest rate discounts to influence the investment levels that firms demand. Suppose it wants all sectors to invest more than they would at the laissez-faire Walrasian equilibrium: it has determined that the Walrasian investment levels are socially suboptimal. It wants citizens to save more and firms to invest more. It announces discounts on the interest rate at which firms can borrow. This will increase the demand for investment by firms, in different amounts, depending on how big the discount is by sector. But now investment demand will outstrip savings of citizens, and so the market interest rate will rise. At equilibrium, if one exists, savings equals investment, and so the central bank will suffer a deficit, since it borrows at the market rate (from citizens) and lends at low rates (to firms). The deficit is financed by corporate taxes. This is only a very approximate explanation of what happens, since in general all other prices will change to equilibrate markets when the market interest rate changes from its value at the Walrasian equilibrium. That is why a mathematical argument is necessary, both to prove that such Lange equilibria in fact exist and to understand what they look like.

From the viewpoint of the theory of economic planning, what is of interest is that what I have called the Lange mechanism—the use of interest rate discounts and surcharges to guide investment—is essentially as powerful a method for influencing investment as some other methods are, including those which would involve much deeper intervention in the economy by the central planning bureau. Consider two other methods. In the first, which we call the *command/market* mechanism, the center commands each firm to purchase a certain specified amount of the investment good. After these commands have been issued, there is no further intervention; markets reach an equilibrium at which all orders are realized and all other markets clear. All firms maximize profits subject to their investment constraints in this model, although it may be that some firms realize negative profits at the equilibrium. (They are not allowed to shut down, for this would entail investing a zero amount, less than the amount they were ordered to invest.) These losses will be covered by subsidies from the center, financed out of taxes on total corporate profits.

The second mechanism we call the *direct-investment* mechanism. In this case, the center issues no commands but it purchases the investment good on the open market and gives it to firms in specified amounts. Firms are free to purchase more of the investment good if they wish, but they may not sell their government grants of investment to other firms. Again, a market equilibrium is reached.

It must be noted that all three of these planning mechanisms make extensive use of markets: prices vary freely and settle when supply equals demand. It may seem that the government would have greater control by using the command/market mechanism or the direct-investment mechanism than by using the Lange mechanism, since it appears to intervene more deeply or directly in the economic process under those two mechanisms. But we have proved that this is not the case. The Lange mechanism can implement more investment vectors than the direct-investment mechanism, and exactly the same set of investment vectors as the command/market mechanism, while maintaining nonnegative social dividends for all citizens.

Furthermore, the Lange mechanism is superior to the other two mechanisms on grounds of informational simplicity. For to give firms the correct commands under the command/market mechanism, or the correct investment grants under the direct-investment mechanism, the center must know the technology of *each* firm; but to use the Lange mechanism, the center need only monitor the total investment orders in an industry and adjust the interest rate discounts or surcharges accordingly, much as the Federal Reserve Bank of the United States adjusts the interest rate it charges to banks. Guiding the economy by the use of interest rates requires less knowledge on the center's part. We therefore view this result as a significant one for the possibility of investment planning in market socialism, that is, for replacing highly centralized administrative systems with "indirect" planning.

In a Lange equilibrium, citizens' incomes are more equal than in a capitalist Walrasian equilibrium because the profits of firms are distributed more equally. Total incomes, however, will not be equal: differences due to differential values of labor remain, as wages are determined by the market. If one wants to alter the distribution of income even more, one must introduce further taxation and transfer payments. Let us note some additional properties of Lange equilibria. The state sets no quantities and arranges for the delivery of no firm's output to any retail outlet, nor does it arrange any investment transactions. All orders, demands and supplies, are decentralized to the firm level; firms acquire all inputs and dispose of all outputs on markets. Firms maximize profits, facing market prices and interest rates, and no firm is subsidized by the government. The center sets no prices, except the interest rate discounts. In the Soviet Union, there were thousands, perhaps hundreds of thousands, of prices set by the center—not to speak of the quantities that were also set, including the planned output of every large firm.

What about efficiency? It can be proved that a Lange equilibrium enjoys the following kind of optimality: there is no technologically feasible allocation of resources that can bring a higher utility to every citizen, given that society shall invest as it has. It is perhaps worthwhile to emphasize that this kind of efficiency comes about because the public firms are maximizing profits; were firms controlled by workers who decided to maximize income per worker, rather than profits, the interest-rate mechanism would not lead to the kind of efficiency that is characteristic of Lange equilibria.[4]

A basic challenge to any model of investment planning is that some political process must be used to choose the investment targets, and this opens up the Pandora's box of rent-seeking, the wasteful use of resources by interest groups who aim to influence the outcome of that process. It is beyond the scope of this essay to engage this challenge. My more modest goals in this section and the previous one have been to show that investment planning can be both beneficial and possible in a market context. Its potential social costs have not been studied. Another challenge is what I listed in §4 as Hayek's third criticism of planning, that it would lead to totalitarianism. The history of planning in market economies belies this prediction.

Taiwan is often held to be a prototype for the effectiveness of free-market economic development. As Robert Wade (1990) effectively argues, however, nothing could be further from the truth. The Taiwanese success story is a story of deep central intervention in the investment process, orchestrated by the Ministries of Finance and Economic Affairs.

The banks in Taiwan are virtually all publicly owned. The four private banks, in 1980, held only 5 percent of total deposits (Wade, 1990, p. 161). Furthermore, private firms are highly leveraged: in the 1980s, about 80 percent of gross private capital formation was bank-financed (as opposed to equity-financed). Since the 1950s, government ministries have issued lists of six to twelve industries annually to the public banks for investment targeting. In the 1970s, the banks themselves began to participate in constructing the lists. Nicholas Riegg writes:

> The banks have taken pride in achieving a high degree of compliance with the lists. With up to 75 percent of loans flowing to the targeted industries it seems that the lists have been an effective means of guiding bank-financed development. Furthermore, as over 80 percent of bank lending goes to the private sector, the lists have obviously helped to guide private enterprise towards the goals of development plans. (Riegg, 1978, p. 96, as quoted in Wade, 1990, p. 167)

There are several mechanisms through which investment targeting has been implemented; prominent among them are low-interest-rate loans subsidized by the government (the Lange mechanism). In addition to regular bank loans, other special funds have been created to target credit allocation. Interest rates were set several points below prevailing bank rates, with long repayment and grace periods (Wade, 1990, p. 167). Another fund gives concessionary loans to firms purchasing domestically manufactured machinery. In 1982, a Strategic Industry Fund (or Preferential Loan Scheme for Strategic and Important Industries) was established, to encourage purchase of domestically produced machinery, or the purchase of new machinery from any source by "strategic" industries, and to encourage automation on a case-by-case basis. The general purpose of the fund, set up after the second oil crisis, was to encourage industry to diversify into less energy-intensive manufacturing. Not only was there a preferential interest rate for these loans, but the payback period was extended to eight years, and a two-year grace period was allowed, generous terms by Taiwanese standards.

Yet another fund (the Sino-American Fund for Economic and Social Development), established in 1965, is directed toward other goals: it promotes pollution control, family planning programs, industrial park development, and industrial technology research institutes. About one-third of its disbursements have been direct grants, the rest being loans at concessionary rates. And the Development Fund is intended to subsidize projects in "technology-intensive and important enterprises, as indicated in the economic plan." About 70 percent of these funds have gone to the private sector, the rest to the public sector. Most of these funds have taken the form of loans, with the interest rate decided case by case, but some have been used to purchase government equity in firms.

Wade (p. 170) concludes that it is difficult to give a precise assessment of how important preferential financing has been in altering the allocation of investment—it has been less important in Taiwan, he writes, than in South Korea. He notes that between 1962 and 1974, the central bank's "special" rediscounted loans to public banks constituted about one-half of its total loans to the banking sector. These loans, of course, could then be made available to firms at lower-than-market interest rates. For my purposes, the Taiwanese example is salient for demonstrating the feasibility of a public banking system as a conduit for influencing the investment policies of a developing country where resources are principally allocated through the market. The methods used have primarily been those of the Lange model I have described—subsidizing investment through preferential interest rates and long payback periods. As well, the direct-investment model has been used, when grants have been made to firms. A third method used in Taiwan, one that I did not discuss in this section, has been government purchase of equity in private firms.

§13

Socialism and democracy

Almost all socialists in the Western world today are democrats; some, such as Samuel Bowles and Herbert Gintis (1986), are interested in socialism in large part only insofar as it is instrumental for bringing about democracy. In §1 I said that one of the things socialists want is equal opportunity for political influence, and I shall here be conventional in assuming that democracy is a precondition for political equality, although this assumption is by no means obviously true. It may be more accurate to say that serious disagreements exist with respect to what form of democracy can deliver the desired equality.[1]

The insistence on democracy has important implications for the socialism of the future, and it will involve a change in the language we use to describe socialism. In a democracy, socialism will be represented by one or several political parties that compete for power with other political parties, some of which will be "bourgeois." It may be the case, sometimes, that a regime could be described as socialist for many years, despite the occasional victories of bourgeois parties. We can say that the Scandinavian countries have remained social-democratic despite occasional victories of oppositional parties.

But the situation of the Sandinistas may be another pattern. A socialist party comes to power. For various reasons—its own errors, the imperialist policies of the United States—it loses the elections some years later and is replaced by a bourgeois party or coalition that undoes a number of its accomplishments. Then perhaps some years later the socialists again win the elections. In this case, we must transform our language from "countries being socialist" to "socialist parties being in power." Perhaps the Sandinistas would not have made some of the errors they did had they thought of themselves as a socialist party in power rather than as the leaders of a socialist country.

Nevertheless, a regime of market socialism might well be characterized by its constitution, which might limit the permissible degree of accumulation of private property in productive assets and perhaps explicitly describe other kinds of property that are (constitutionally) protected. One justification for a supermajoritarian requirement to reverse such provisions is that property relations will not engender long-term planning and, in particular, investment if they are thought to be easily reversible; another is that large social costs would be sustained in any change in property relations.

I think it is incontrovertible that a key reform necessary to achieve the equality of opportunity desired by socialists is massively improved education for the children of the poor and working class. Only through education can the difference in opportunities faced by them and the children of the well-off be eradicated; only when skills become less unequally distributed, because of education, will wage differentials narrow significantly. Reaching a consensus to devote the required amount of resources to this kind of education will require a massive change in outlook of the citizenry of every large, heterogeneous country. Majorities will have to overcome their racism, but more than that, they will have to be won over to John Donne's view that "No man is an island entire of itself." The implementation of a thorough-going socialism in a democracy will take a long time, then, if it must await such a feeling of community among people.

But I think that a market-socialist system would cure a number of the ills of capitalism more quickly, without the prerequisite of this feeling of community, because of the changed economic interests people would have under the various proposals for property redistribution that I have cited. I have outlined how the level of various public bads in a democratic society is the outcome of a political struggle in which different classes fight for their interests. If interests change, then so, in general, will the equilibrium level of public bads.

Let me take as an example the Persian Gulf war of 1991. A case can be made that that war was fought to keep the price of oil low, and that the main interests who wanted the price of oil kept low were firms using oil as an input. Of course, all consumers want a low price of oil: the question is, who was willing to go to war in January 1991 to keep the price of oil low, and who would have been content to apply a boycott for another year? As late as December 15, 1990, one month prior to the U.S.-led air raids on Iraq, surveys taken in the United States showed that the great majority of people were opposed to starting a war. One can take this as evidence that they were willing to trade off the possibility of a somewhat higher price for oil and a somewhat higher rate of unemployment for not going to war. Yet President Bush decided to go to war, and in doing so he probably had support from "important people"—those who derive huge amounts of wealth from profits of firms, those for whom the fall in profits that would ensue from higher oil prices made the alternative of war a preferable one.[2]

Now suppose that in a market-socialist economy no one received more than roughly a per-capita share of total profits. A rise in the price of oil would, of course, hurt profits and wages, but, arguably, no class of "important people" would have such an overwhelming interest in keeping oil prices low. Almost everyone might prefer to take the chance of higher oil prices to avoid having to fight a war.

If many of the ills of capitalism are public bads of this kind—bads that increase profits—then, even if the preference orderings (for noneconomists: values) of individuals do not change, a change in the distribution of profit income would change the level of public bads that is engendered by a democratic process. I think that, to some extent, racism and sexism are public bads of this kind. An old Marxist argument maintains that divisions among the working class—created, for example, by racism and sexism— strengthen the bosses in the struggle against labor.[3] To the extent that this is the case, capitalism may develop mechanisms to foment racism and sexism, for example, by the treatment of minorities and women in the capitalist media. The public-bad argument of §7 implies that, were profits equally distributed in the population, capitalist-inspired divisiveness in the working class would be reduced. I do not ignore the fact that people themselves have racist and sexist ideas, and so one cannot expect changes overnight with respect to these practices. But the change in property relations would dissolve one powerful class interest in the maintenance of discrimination.

A fundamental left-wing criticism of capitalist democracy has been that, as long as capital is in the hands of a small, wealthy class, politics must conform to the needs of that class. (See, for instance, Block, 1977, and Przeworski, 1985,

p. 42.) With public bank directors popularly elected and legal provisions limiting the freedom of firms to export capital, the "structural power of capital" over society as a whole would be broken. Those who control capital would not be able to hold society hostage by threatening to take the means of production (and the jobs that go with it) overseas. In his proposal, Block (1992) accomplishes this result by requiring the boards of directors that oversee banks to represent a variety of constituencies, including citizens who are not shareholders.

It would be comforting to be able to argue that, once a mechanism for redistributing profits, or for transforming firms into labor-managed ones, had been put in place, then a feeling of community would eventually develop and the well-to-do would be willing to sacrifice income in order to fund the kind of educational system that would open up opportunities for those currently shut out of the system. I do not see the evidence for this claim. Despite the fact of significant egalitarianism in the European social democracies, that degree of community has not developed there. The ideology of individualism appears to remain quite strong, as reflected in the resurgence of the conservative parties. Despite the norm of egalitarianism that existed to a nontrivial extent in Yugoslavia, the Eastern European countries, and the U.S.S.R., we do not see a powerful socialist phoenix rising from the ashes of Communism.

This brings up the question whether the transformation from individualistic values to socialist values—the making of the "socialist man," as many used to say—will be facilitated by institutions of market socialism or whether, indeed, such a transformation will ever occur. Every socialist revolution (the Soviet Union, China, Cuba) has had its golden age, a period when a large fraction of the population was motivated to sacrifice in the name of building socialism and otherwise behave in a cooperative manner. But these golden ages have been quite short; it is not clear whether these periods of cooperation would have continued if the states had enjoyed continued economic success or whether the golden spirit cannot last, regardless of economic accomplishments, because, for instance, it is engendered by a great *change* for the better rather than a period of *stable* good times.[4]

I therefore remain agnostic on the question of a wholesale change in human nature. I prefer to put my faith in the design of institutions that will bring about good results with ordinary people. Having confessed to a certain agnosticism, would I nevertheless admit the possibility that market socialism would eventually increase the support for, say, greater expenditures on public education? Perhaps: again, I will invoke the public-bad argument. To a degree, education of the working class is a profit-increasing public good, and to this degree, it is rational for capitalists to support its financing. It is almost certainly the case that publicly supported education in the United States is at present below this degree, and indeed significant sections of the capitalist class support increased educational funding: U.S. workers would be more productive and could more easily acquire profit-enhancing skills if they could read detailed instruction manuals, as Japanese workers can.[5]

It may well be the case, however, that the optimal degree of working-class education for capitalists is less than the socially optimal degree—after a point, that is, increased public education may have a net negative effect on profits (when the taxes on profits needed to finance the marginal educational increment for the working class are more than the profits the increment induces), although it may continue to have a large positive marginal effect as a public good via its effect on social culture (in which I include

everything from improved television programming to public civility). It is this additional educational increment which,
according to the argument of §7, a society in which profits
are equally distributed is more likely to support through its
political process.[6]

I have not thus far addressed in this essay what is the
largest injustice in the world, the massive inequality between nations, conveniently described as North-South inequality. In the next fifty years, however, it may well be this
inequality which becomes the focus of politics: as the South
industrializes, it may well demand large transfers from the
North to enable it to do so without destroying the global
commons. I have no doubt that such transfers are required
by justice, for where one is born is a morally arbitrary personal feature, and equality of opportunity mandates compensation to those born into societies with low standards of
living. The question is whether a market-socialist society
would be more prone to support such transfers than a capitalist one.

The practices of the Scandinavian countries suggest perhaps the answer is yes; foreign aid is a larger fraction of
national income in Norway and Sweden than in any other
country, and this appears to be due to the effect of socialist
values.[7] The social-democratic parties in Scandinavia have
advocated relatively large development aid on grounds of
solidarity. Furthermore, there is evidence that many people
in industrialized countries advocate divestment of corporate
stock in South Africa: here is a case where people are willing
to sacrifice a small amount of income (in the form of slightly
higher wages, profits, and pensions that are possible with
South African investment) for the sake of the freedom of
people in a distant land. It is therefore not absurd to suggest
that the low welfare of people in the South is a (profit-
inducing) public bad, as far as many people in the North are

concerned, and as such, foreign aid might well increase with a redistribution of profits.

It is important to bear in mind the distinction between two causes of policy change (with regard to education, foreign aid, and other matters) that we might observe in a market-socialist society: (1) those changes in political outcomes that are due to changing property relations but occur in the face of unchanging preference orderings (or values) of individuals, and (2) those changes that are due to changing preference orderings of individuals. The public-bads argument of §7 that I have exploited here assumes unchanging values, though I do think that values change as people experience new situations. And so if, for example, public funding of education increases, at first for purely practical reasons having to do with the need for more highly skilled workers, it is possible that the new equilibrium, where people are better educated, may well induce a value change, which then would bring about further increases in educational funding. I do believe, however, that value changes occur slowly, and by no means do they always occur in the "right" direction. Albert Hirschman (1982) has argued that values cycle between a focus on the public and a focus on the private. For these reasons, I do not base a blueprint for a socialist future on the evolution of the selfless individual.

§14

Criticisms of market socialism from the left

The left has made several powerful challenges to both labor-managed market socialism and managerial market socialism. Perhaps the most basic objection is the claim that competition is responsible for some of capitalism's fundamental shortcomings and that these would therefore be inherited by all varieties of market socialism, because they too rely on competition among firms.

Where there is competition, there are losers, and where there are losers, there is often loss of self-esteem. If self-esteem is what Rawls (1971) calls a primary good, and arguably one of the most important, what progress toward human fulfillment would be made by a market socialism that preserved the division of the world into winners and losers? Now it does not necessarily follow that a society whose economic mechanism requires competition of business enterprises also requires that kind of interpersonal competitiveness whose result is the loss of self-esteem for those who lose. Yet an argument can be made, I think, that competition in the economic sphere engenders interpersonal competition as a more generalized phenomenon in society. But even without such an argument, it must be the case that, as long as markets are used to allocate labor, people will in large part measure themselves by the income they earn. (As a *New Yorker* cartoon quipped, "Money is life's report card.")

Another consequence of competition is a lack of community. As G. A. Cohen (1991) writes, the market "motivates contribution not on the basis of commitment to one's fellow human beings, but on the basis of impersonal cash reward." Nevertheless, to the extent that market socialism increases equality of income, it will increase community, which is fostered, *inter alia*, by equality of condition.

A second criticism from the left arises from the view, associated with Bowles and Gintis (1986) and Cohen and Rogers (1983, 1993), that what is principally valuable about socialism is its extension of democracy into economic life. Managerial market socialism, which does not even introduce industrial democracy, is a weak advance at best over capitalism.

The substantive issue posed by these challenges is whether the market-socialist proposals I have outlined represent sufficient advances over capitalism to be called "socialist" in the egalitarian sense described in §1. I have tried to make the distinction between short-term and long-term proposals, and I intend market socialism as a short-term proposal: to wit, I do not defend as just any system in which people receive wages proportional to their acquired skills, imprinted as the distribution of skill is and will be for many decades or even centuries to come with the weave of its ancestor, unequal opportunity. The salient issue is: Does there exist a next step from capitalism approaching the long-term socialist goal that is better than some variety of market socialism?[1] It will come as no surprise that I believe there is not, although I have no proof.

I have no objection to further redistribution of income through social-democratic methods—in effect, this means by the provision of more goods through public financing and its associated system of progressive taxation. I have registered my skepticism with regard to the applicability of the Nordic social-democratic model to the world as a whole. Here, I mention another caveat. In a market economy, I think people tend to believe they have earned, in the moral sense, what they receive through selling their talents on the market. (A closely related claim is that market competition engenders a loss of self-esteem for those who are not economically successful.) This view is raised to high principle by liberal philosophy of the Lockean variety, which argues that people have a right to keep that which they make by their wits and brawn;[2] it is unfortunate that many Marxists who define exploitation by invoking the labor theory of value implicitly commit themselves to a similar moral stand.[3] Although modern egalitarian political philosophy is clearly in disagreement with this liberal view, it is, perhaps, psychologically mandated in people who compete on labor markets. If so, this places a political limit on the degree of redistribution that can be accomplished by social-democratic methods: an economic mechanism, at least in a democracy, cannot be stable if it rewards people in disproportion to what they believe they deserve. Indeed, the current semi-reversion of Scandinavian social democracy to a less egalitarian capitalism may have this psychological fact as one source.

Another mechanism for redistribution whose use I support is estate taxes. From the viewpoint of justice, high estate taxes are doubly justified. First, to the extent that differential earnings and savings are in large part due to the unequal distribution of opportunities for earning and saving, estate taxes are justified by the need to ensure equality of opportunity. Second, even if people have justly earned (under conditions of equal opportunity) their estates, it does not follow that they have the right to exacerbate differential opportunities in the next generation by distributing their estates to favored individuals. The requirement of equality of opportunity for the next generation may well trump such a right.

Why are estate taxes so low in capitalist countries? Doubtless, the rates are low in part because of lobbying by the wealthy, but also because, in market economies, people feel that they have justly earned what they acquire through market exchange, and that they therefore have a right to dispense with their estates as they choose. There is also the less lofty reason: many people who would enjoy net benefits from much higher estate taxes entertain a possibility that is statistically highly improbable—that they will themselves strike it rich, in which case estate taxes would be personally harmful. These same motivations would, in all likelihood, afflict many people in a market-socialist economy in which labor markets were important, and so redistribution through estate taxes may not be politically much more feasible under market socialism than it is under capitalism.

The limited degree of equality that I think market socialism can achieve is due in the main to my skepticism concerning the existence of alternatives to a competitive labor market for allocating labor in an efficient manner. Indeed, the key to the market-socialist proposals outlined in this essay is the fundamental asymmetry between wages and profits as categories of national income: while considerations of efficiency pretty much determine the distribution of wages among workers,[4] they do not so determine the distribution of profits. There is, as I claimed in §1, a degree of freedom in the distribution of profits, even if we hold constant the overall level of economic efficiency. This view is predicated on the estimate that the extreme concentration of profits that is characteristic of capitalist societies is not due to the possession and exercise, by the few, of talents that are as scarce in the population as their remuneration under capitalism would seem to imply. Or, the view can also be predicated on the estimate that, although extremely scarce, those talents would nevertheless be exercised, even by their self-interested holders, with substantially less remuneration than they receive under capitalist property relations.

To the objection that competition and its bad effects remain present in the market-socialist models I have proposed, my response is pragmatic. I think the Soviet experience has shown us that even an authoritarian politico-economic mechanism, *a fortiori* a democratic one, cannot be stable for a society unless it delivers to its members goods of comparable quality to those available in other societies similar in culture and educational achievement. Thus, socialist politico-economic mechanisms must be capable of innovation at roughly the rate sustained by capitalist ones. This claim about popular demands is an empirical one, based on a small sample. But we do know that the Soviet authorities argued tenaciously that people should value the security of life under Communism over the variety of life under capitalism. Surely, Soviet citizens did not fully comprehend the degree of insecurity of life under capitalism. But, for the same reason, one can predict that a market-socialist society would not be stable if it failed to give its citizens roughly the variety that capitalism provides. As I have argued, we know of no mechanism that can produce an innovative economy except interfirm competition, and it follows that we must limit our investigation to models based upon such competition.

Those who believe capitalism's fundamental evil is the competitive spirit it induces in people may well say, if they accept my argument, that the game is not worth the candle. But I furthermore believe that, even should community and self-esteem be compromised by competition, the market-socialist proposals, if enacted, would still mark progress toward a just society. The improvement in the distribution of wealth and income and the reduction in public bads that they would bring, if the theory is correct, would greatly increase the opportunities for self-realization and welfare of those who would have been much worse off under capitalism. The evidence for this claim comes from the Nordic countries.

Finally, I offer a defense of the managerial market-socialist model against those who argue that labor management must be a feature of the next step. As I have noted in §6, contemporary models of labor-managed market socialism all recognize that firms must raise capital from nonmembers, either through a stock market or through bank loans, and this would, to some unknown extent, compromise the autonomy of workers with regard to control of the firm. It is therefore not clear to what extent the managerial and labor-managed proposals for market socialism really differ. My preference for the managerial proposals is based on conservatism, namely, that it is best to change features of a system one at a time, if possible.[5] The biological metaphor is apt: an organism with one mutation is more likely to survive than one in which two mutations occur simultaneously. I think it is more important to change the private nature of the financing of firms than the management structure as the first step. Of course, I am assuming that we are beginning from an economy whose firms have a hierarchical structure of management. If we begin with an economy in which workers have substantial management power, then that, too, should be retained in the first step. This may, for example, be the case in many firms in the former Soviet Union.

This last point should not be taken to imply that I unequivocally endorse introducing labor management as the second step after financial restructuring has been successfully completed, for labor management may make firms too risk-averse, as several authors have noted.[6] It may, for instance, be socially optimal for firms to take a degree of risk that results in the likelihood that each worker will have to change jobs, say, three or four times in her working life, because of a layoff or bankruptcy. But individuals might well wish to avoid even this degree of risk.

Indeed, it is possible that adopting the form of labor management for all firms in an economy could have the result that everyone is worse off than they would be in an economy with mixed management forms. Suppose that labor-managed firms are, without external provocation, more risk-averse than managerial firms, and hence engender fewer innovations. Suppose all firms but mine have adopted labor management. It may be optimal for workers in my firm to vote for labor management as well: for if we chose the alternative, the traditional managerial form, there would be insufficient competition from the other labor-managed firms to induce our firm to innovate, and so we gain nothing by choosing to remain under traditional management. But the equilibrium reached when all firms are managed by labor may well be suboptimal, because of the low degree of innovation that would result: perhaps all would prefer to sacrifice the autonomy they have under labor management for the higher living standards associated (by assumption) with an economy containing a sufficiently large number of managerial firms. If the claim about the excessive risk-aversion of labor-managed firms is true, it seems that the optimal arrangement would be an economy containing, in addition to the labor-managed firms, a sufficient number of managerial firms to induce a desirable rate of innovation.[7]

§15

Prospects for the future

Writing obituaries for socialism is a popular pastime these days. It was utopian, the critics say, to believe a society could be founded on a norm of egalitarianism. Greed is good, they say, or at least it is a necessary evil, a motivating force that can be tamed by the right institutions—the market, contract law, private property—to bring about the material conditions enabling human dignity and fulfillment for all.

While the end of the Soviet Union is to be welcomed to the extent that we would applaud the fall of any tyrannical state, its demise also marks a setback for socialism: for many hundreds of millions of people, its existence reinforced the belief that, though not yet a reality, a society based on a norm of equality could be more than just a dream. And holding that belief is a precondition for struggling to create such a society. This essay's aim has been to sketch blueprints for a feasible socialism, to provide a basis, once again, for daring to believe in the dream.

At the least, I hope readers will take away from this essay two crucial ideas. The first is the view that the goal of socialism is best thought of as a kind of egalitarianism, not the implementation of a specific property relation. I am saying, in other words, that property relations must be evaluated by socialists with respect to their ability to deliver that kind of egalitarianism. The Soviet experiment was only one of various conceivable experiments, and its failure does not impeach the possibility of more successful attempts. There is ample reason to believe that the failure of Soviet systems is ascribable not to the egalitarian goals of Communism but to the abrogation of markets and, therefore, to the loss of incentives and competition that followed.

The second idea is that modern capitalism provides us with many fertile possibilities for designing the next wave of socialist experiments. Modern capitalism owes its relative success, in bringing about economic growth, to legal environments and cultures that engender competition and to its ability to devise mechanisms capable of solving agency problems. It does not, in particular, owe its success specifically to its embrace of the right to unlimited accumulation of private property, except insofar as that right may be inseparable from the characteristics just named. But modern capitalism itself illustrates that such a right is not essential to its success, for the modern capitalist corporation, unlike the firm of its ancestor described by Adam Smith and Friedrich Hayek, does not function by virtue of the genius of a single man, to whom all profits flow. The diffusion of profits in the modern corporation is, by comparison with the operation of firms in early capitalism, extreme. To accomplish that degree of diffusion, without sacrificing the efficiency and inventiveness of the firm, modern capitalism has employed a variety of devices, and I believe that these devices can be successfully employed by a system in which the distribution of profits is a great deal more diffuse than it is in modern capitalism.

At a more general level, the claims of this essay concerning the feasibility of socialism depend upon a distinction between the roles of private property and of markets. As our ideas, and our economic theory, can only be based on history—an infinitely richer source than human imagination—we can have, at this juncture, only a vague conception of the distinctive functions of private property and markets, for until now the two have virtually always appeared together. But we do have several examples—the modern corporation, and perhaps the town and village enterprises in China—that allow us to begin to understand that aspects of economic development which the received theory has attributed to the right to the unfettered accumulation of private property may in fact be due to competition and markets instead. As our understanding of this distinction becomes more concrete—and it will, no doubt, with the continuing evolution of property forms in market economies—the designs of more egalitarian societies will be rendered in sharper focus. In all likelihood, the market-socialist blueprints offered in §§6 and 8 of this essay are primitive, and will continue to evolve. I encourage the reader to take those blueprints as suggestive only, useful as clarifying examples of this general view.

In this final section on the near-term prospects for socialist ideals, I want to avoid adding to the literature of "transitology." Yet for any end state of a social process to be feasible, a path must exist from here to there, and so at least a rough sketch of possible routes, if not a precise map, may reasonably be asked of someone attempting to describe the final destination. I preface the remarks that follow with the caveat that recent history has shown we tread on thin ice when trying to predict the future.

The countries where the opportunity costs of adopting market socialism are the least are, I believe, those that have formed in Eastern/Central Europe and out of the Soviet

Union since 1989. These countries face a momentous task of institution building, no matter what kind of market system they will have, and one could argue that the costs of designing a coupon stock market, a bank-centric monitoring system, and constitutions that adequately shelter economic institutions (banks, firms) from state interference would be no greater than the costs of building a capitalist system along Anglo-American lines. Indeed, Corbett and Mayer (1991) have argued that a monitoring system based on banks would be easier to build in the new republics than one based on decentralized market actors and the takeover process.

Politically, however, the ideological ambience in many of these countries is unfavorable to market socialism: the cry has been, naively, "No more experiments," as if experiments can be avoided in any kind of transition to a market economy. Nevertheless, introducing the kind of market socialism advocated here in some of these states will perhaps be politically possible in a few years, if a substantial sector of state-owned firms is maintained, as I think will be the case in many countries. The experiments in extreme laissez-faire, as perhaps we are now seeing in the Czech republic, are not apt to produce the enlightened capitalism of Sweden or Finland—a more likely result will be the vulgar capitalism of Mexico or Brazil. In countries that maintain large state sectors (perhaps Russia and the Asian Soviet republics, for instance, will do so), political parties that call for a more egalitarian kind of denationalization may in the future gain massive popular support. I think, as well, that this kind of transformation is not out of the question in China or Vietnam, or perhaps in Cuba.

Indeed, the last dozen years have seen the development in China of what may be the first indigenous and competitive form of socialist enterprise, the so-called town and village enterprises (TVEs). These are small, industrial firms that have formed in rural areas, where they compete with state-owned firms. At first they specialized in light industry, but now they also engage in heavy industry. By 1991, there were some 19 million TVEs employing 96 million workers, or about 40 percent of China's industrial employment. While in 1979, when the reform started, agriculture accounted for 70 percent of the value of output in rural areas, it now accounts for about 45 percent. Who owns the TVEs? The answer is vague—ownership forms probably cover the gamut of possibilities, from the disguised private firm in the hands of a few partners to ventures that are genuinely owned by local governments. The profits of TVEs are divided among local infrastructure, investment, and dividends to individual households. According to *The Economist* (November 28, 1992), these enterprises are "ferociously competitive" and operate with hard budget constraints: no state banks are available to bail out losers. Although the overall record is one of amazing growth, some 3 million TVEs failed during the austerity year of 1989. If it is correct that the profits of the TVEs go primarily into financing local public goods, such as schools and roads, then a large part of the transformation of the Chinese economy since 1979, only partially indicated by a real GNP growth rate averaging 9 percent a year since then, will have been due to a new form of property appropriately described as market-socialist.

The three categories of capitalist country are advanced democratic, developing democratic, and developing authoritarian. I think the transformation to market socialism is least likely, in the foreseeable future, in advanced democratic capitalism, for here the laws and institutions that guarantee private property are stable in the sense that they are supported by the overwhelming majority of people. Advanced capitalism is more likely to attenuate class struggle with social-democratic concessions than with nationalization of private assets, unless some massive economic catastrophe occurs, in which case other doors will open as well.

Authoritarian developing countries in which the rate of growth and pattern of distribution of wealth have been insufficient to improve the conditions of a large working and peasant class are candidates for market socialism, especially when extreme material inequality has engendered leftist parties with a popular base: South Africa and El Salvador are perhaps the best examples today. Popular sentiment may support substantial nationalization of private assets should the Left come to power in these countries, and the public sector could then be organized along market-socialist lines. Authoritarian developing capitalist countries with high rates of growth (such as South Korea and Taiwan) are more likely to become democratic capitalist countries in the near future, for those economies have succeeded in dramatically raising the standard of living for almost everyone during the last generation.

Finally, I think the category of developing democratic capitalist countries must also be partitioned into those which have delivered an increasing standard of living to the working class and those which have not. In those countries where the working classes are kept near destitution, leftist parties may be able to make political headway toward a redistribution of wealth. The Partido dos Trabalhadores (PT) in Brazil, for instance, which almost took power in the 1988 elections, and the Party of the Democratic Revolution (PRD) in Mexico, which perhaps did win the elections in 1988 although it did not take power, could conceivably win in future elections on a market-socialist platform and transform the sizable, inefficient state sectors of these economies along the lines that have been described here.

It is not, however, clear that history is on the side of socialism, at least in the short run. As Ken Jowitt (1991) has forcefully argued, the world may be in for a period of disorder as societies already pressured by economic decline are ignited by nationalism. Capitalist reforms in the formerly Communist states will almost surely fail to produce the kind of societies that their citizens observe in Western Europe; they are much more likely to bring about a highly unequal distribution of wealth and massive insecurity for a sizable fraction of the working class. The citizens of these countries will discover that the revolutions of 1989 were stolen from them. These countries will then be ripe for nationalist and fascist movements—as well as for socialist ones. But the potential of any socialist movement depends upon its ability to provide blueprints, especially since the first model of socialist society, the Soviet Union, has failed. (It failed as a model of socialism, but the world may be vastly better off for the fact that it existed, as I indicated in the first paragraph of §3.) Fortunately, this job is not impossible: there are many ideas on how to improve on the old model, lessons learned from the twentieth-century history of both Communism and capitalism.

Morale is a key problem for socialists today: to keep the objective point of view, to understand how brief a moment is seventy years in human history, to remember how continuous has been the struggle of mankind against inequality and injustice, and to realize how enduring are those problems that engendered the socialist idea almost two centuries ago. And it is not as if we have not learned from those seventy years of Soviet experience: we have learned massively. Those who trumpet the theme that capitalism has won, or that we have reached the end of history, reveal only their own myopia. Capitalism may have won, but certainly it is too soon to tell. Recall Zhou Enlai's wise response to a request to comment on the consequences of the French Revolution: "It's too soon to tell." There is still ample reason to believe, as Marx once said, that real human history—the history of society that, for the vast majority of people, has eliminated material scarcity as the unbreachable barrier to self-realization—has not yet begun.

APPENDIX

The value of the coupon dividend in the United States

For the sake of illustration, I present here rough calculations of the profit dividend each adult in the United States would receive if the coupon economy of §8 were operable.[1] These calculations are rough, because a number of magnitudes that I assume would remain fixed would, doubtless, change. I assume that total production of firms would remain fixed, as would the corporate interest rate. To be more exact, what I report here is a reaccounting of the profit income of U.S. firms in the period 1950–1990 to adjust for the fact that, in the coupon economy, citizens would not hold equity in firms: the income flows to citizens that now take the form of dividends would take the form of interest payments to savers, and would not be accounted for as profits, in a coupon economy.

I limit myself to examining the nonfinancial business sector of the economy. (This excludes the financial sector and farms and, for the first set of calculations, noncorporate businesses as well.) What would total profits of the *nonfinancial corporate* sector be if firms' investments were entirely financed by bonds and bank loans, as in the coupon economy, instead of equity? I assume that the present equity of firms in the corporate sector would be transformed into debt, and payment of interest on that debt would be accounted a cost. The profits that would be left over for distribution to coupon holders would be profits after payment of such interest. Thus, let

$\pi^{cap}(t)$ = total pre-tax corporate profits in year t

$E(t)$ = total value of corporate equity in year t

$D(t)$ = net total indebtedness of the corporate sector in year t

$i(t)$ = net interest paid by the corporate sector in year t

$c(t)$ = capital consumption allowance of the corporate sector in year t

$r(t)$ = average rate of interest on corporate debt in year t

$\pi^{coup}(t)$ = total corporate profits in coupon economy

The accounting identity that I use is:

$$\pi^{coup}(t) = \pi^{cap}(t) + c(t) + i(t) - r(t)[D(t) + E(t)]$$

The data for the variables π, E, D, c, and i are taken from the national accounts; $\pi^{coup}(t)$ is the imputed coupon profit figure we wish to estimate. Thus, $\pi^{cap}(t) + c(t) + i(t)$ is the "net surplus" of corporations; from this we subtract our estimate of what total interest payments would be in the coupon economy when equity financing would be replaced by debt.[2]

I estimated $r(t)$ as the effective rate of interest in year t, that is, $r(t) = i(t)/D(t)$. Table A1 reports the *per-adult* value of $\pi^{coup}(t)$ since 1950, in current dollars (that is, unadjusted for inflation). The remarkable fact is that these values are not appreciably higher in recent years than they were in the 1950s, and so in real terms, they are much lower in recent times. The third column of Table A1 lists the median annual income of black males (in current dollars) in the United States, while the last column lists the ratio of the per-adult dividend to that income. In the 1950s, the coupon dividend would have constituted a substantial increase—about 20 percent over the decade—in the median income of black males. (We may view this dividend as a net *addition* to income, as median black males owned essentially no corporate stock in the 1950s.) In the 1980s, however, the coupon dividend would never have constituted more than 7 percent of median black income. (I use median black income as a proxy for the poverty level. Median black female income was one-third of median black male income in 1950 and only 65 percent of black male income by 1990. These coupon dividends would represent a dramatically greater fraction of median black female income.)

The value of $\pi^{coup}(t)$ as calculated from the equation used here may, for several reasons, underestimate what the true value of the coupon dividend would be. First, depreciation rules were liberalized in the 1970s, and perhaps the capital consumption adjustment is not sufficient to bring reported profits up to true economic profits. Table A2 reports the ratio of taxable depreciation to capital stock of the nonfinancial corporate sector by year; note the increase in this ratio from the mid-1970s on. Second, a portion of what is

Table A1. Per-adult coupon dividends, variant 1

Year	Dividend per adult	Median income of black males	Ratio
1950	$336.938	$1344.79	0.250552
1951	332.962	1565.35	0.212708
1952	280.345	1634.36	0.171532
1953	296.015	1725.11	0.171592
1954	259.784	1540.53	0.168633
1955	358.319	1711.89	0.209311
1956	344.186	1837.3	0.187333
1957	321.958	1898.09	0.169622
1958	239.908	1824.82	0.131469
1959	319.128	1816.08	0.175724
1960	289.409	2086.34	0.138716
1961	269.137	2107.49	0.127705
1962	336.455	2106.46	0.159725
1963	366.002	2291.63	0.159712
1964	405.462	2571.95	0.157647
1965	477.868	2613.44	0.18285
1966	519.598	2854.63	0.18202
1967	431.472	3065.35	0.140758
1968	446.166	3423.79	0.130313
1969	411.071	3664.61	0.112173

Table A1 (continued).

Year	Dividend per adult	Median income of black males	Ratio
1970	261.537	3902.79	0.0670128
1971	282.706	4044.05	0.0699066
1972	340.296	4450.07	0.0764698
1973	531.649	4824.67	0.110194
1974	608.791	5212.33	0.116798
1975	474.924	5332.6	0.0890605
1976	625.582	5723.42	0.109302
1977	777.107	6051.1	0.128424
1978	886.833	6606.17	0.134243
1979	833.527	7462.56	0.111695
1980	493.22	8046.4	0.0612969
1981	459.916	8609.47	0.0534197
1982	60.3233	8927.31	0.00675716
1983	331.809	8994.71	0.0368893
1984	644.053	9459.32	0.0680866
1985	549.372	10744.2	0.051132
1986	310.242	10783.	0.0287715
1987	701.938	11176.5	0.0628048
1988	820.794	12073.2	0.0679848
1989	310.414	12654.9	0.0245291

Table A2. Depreciation as a fraction of capital stock

Year	Ratio	Year	Ratio
1950	0.0671517	1970	0.0646597
1951	0.0707692	1971	0.0661783
1952	0.0697127	1972	0.0684544
1953	0.0683391	1973	0.0681205
1954	0.0671492	1974	0.0727273
1955	0.0665421	1975	0.0803136
1956	0.0686813	1976	0.0819345
1957	0.0694225	1977	0.0833696
1958	0.0683507	1978	0.0855744
1959	0.0672808	1979	0.0881908
1960	0.0657068	1980	0.0900676
1961	0.0637667	1981	0.0950023
1962	0.0625	1982	0.0950292
1963	0.0614267	1983	0.0920276
1964	0.0605998	1984	0.0859888
1965	0.0601923	1985	0.0817108
1966	0.0605684	1986	0.0798339
1967	0.0615512	1987	0.0777499
1968	0.062844	1988	0.0773323
1969	0.0634697	1989	0.0777833

reported as nonfinancial, noncorporate business income in the national accounts is income not, in fact, of small businesses (that would not be in the coupon sector) but of large firms that would, perhaps, be in the coupon sector under market socialism. Hughes Aircraft, for instance, is a nonincorporated business. Corporations that "went private" through leveraged buyouts in the 1980s will also be in this category. Nonfinancial, noncorporate business income in 1990 was $360 billion, while total corporate profits were $232 billion. Perhaps more striking is the statistic that the wealthiest one-half of one percent of U.S. households in 1989 owned corporate stock valued at $327 billion, while the value of their noncorporate business holdings was $1,500 billion. Indeed, there has been a rapid shift toward unincorporated business holdings in the type of assets held by the very wealthy; in 1983, they held $516 billion in corporate stock and $849 billion in noncorporate business. These statistics suggest that a fraction of noncorporate business income consists in very large holdings that would be nationalized under market socialism.

Table A3 reports the results of a second calculation of the per-adult coupon dividend, where two adjustments are made to take account of these two phenomena. In the period 1950–1974 inclusive, the average rate of depreciation, calculated from Table A2, was .0656. For the period 1975–1990, I define excess depreciation[3] as:

$$x(t) = dpr(t) - .0656K(t)$$

where $dpr(t)$ is reported taxable depreciation in year t and $K(t)$ is total capital stock of the nonfinancial corporate sector in year t. Thus, $x(t)$ is the excess of depreciation in year t over what it would have been had depreciation been calculated at the historical rate of the period 1950–1974. To

Table A3. Per-adult coupon dividends, variant 2

Year	Dividend per adult	Median income of black males	Ratio
1950	$426.7	$1344.79	0.317299
1951	430.704	1565.35	0.27515
1952	381.705	1634.36	0.23355
1953	399.961	1725.11	0.231847
1954	364.842	1540.53	0.236829
1955	471.067	1711.89	0.275173
1956	461.663	1837.3	0.251273
1957	445.013	1898.09	0.234453
1958	364.586	1824.82	0.199794
1959	449.374	1816.08	0.247442
1960	417.132	2086.34	0.199935
1961	400.454	2107.49	0.190015
1962	471.956	2106.46	0.224051
1963	503.903	2291.63	0.219888
1964	552.505	2571.95	0.214819
1965	629.901	2613.44	0.241024
1966	678.392	2854.63	0.237647
1967	595.893	3065.35	0.194397
1968	616.659	3423.79	0.18011
1969	584.34	3664.61	0.159455

Table A3 (continued).

Year	Dividend per adult	Median income of black males	Ratio
1970	434.307	3902.79	0.111281
1971	465.195	4044.05	0.115032
1972	536.676	4450.07	0.120599
1973	740.915	4824.67	0.153568
1974	880.006	5212.33	0.168832
1975	822.83	5332.6	0.154302
1976	1028.06	5723.42	0.179623
1977	1232.27	6051.1	0.203643
1978	1409.37	6606.17	0.213342
1979	1424.15	7462.56	0.190839
1980	1136.18	8046.4	0.141203
1981	1206.68	8609.47	0.140157
1982	840.296	8927.31	0.0941264
1983	1142.86	8994.71	0.127059
1984	1442.33	9459.32	0.152477
1985	1335.83	10744.2	0.12433
1986	1094.95	10783.	0.101544
1987	1488.24	11176.5	0.133158
1988	1635.48	12073.2	0.135464
1989	1165.52	12654.9	0.0921004

address the second qualification, I assumed that 30 percent of nonfinancial business income would, in the coupon economy, become income of the coupon sector. (I cannot easily find data on the distribution of nonfinancial, noncorporate income by size of firm, but I assume that this income is fairly concentrated, so that 30 percent of it is probably earned by very large firms.) Let $nfb(t)$ be nonfinancial, noncorporate business income in year t, net of depreciation and interest payments; then the more liberal calculation of the coupon dividend, as presented in Table A3, is calculated by the accounting identity:

$$\pi^{coup}(t) = \pi^{cap}(t) + c(t) + i(t) + x(t)$$
$$+ .3nfb(t) - r(t)[D(t) + E(t)]$$

With this accounting, we see that the adult dividend would have been about 25 percent of black median income in the 1950s and about 12 percent of that income on average in the 1980s.

At least according to these rough calculations, it appears that for a period of postwar history in the United States, the coupon dividend would have dramatically increased the income of the poor and radically altered the distribution of income. In developing countries, where profits generally constitute a much higher fraction of national income than they do in the United States, the same would be true. The profitability of the nonfinancial sector in the United States has fallen in recent years, and this is reflected in a decrease of the per-adult coupon dividend. In fact, it may be the case that profits have shifted in the direction of the financial sector, whose profits I have not accounted for in these calculations. If, under market socialism, the profits of the financial sector were returned mainly to the treasury, then the average citizen would benefit from the publicly provided goods that would be financed by them, a welfare increment I have here ignored.

Sources

The series $\pi^{cap}(t)$, $c(t)$, and $dpr(t)$ were taken from Table F.104 of the *Flow of Funds Accounts, 1945–1990*, published by the Federal Reserve System (March 10, 1993). The series $D(t)$ and $E(t)$ were taken from the same publication, Tables L.2 and L.215, respectively. The series $i(t)$ was acquired directly from the Federal Reserve. The series $K(t)$ was taken from Table A8, p. 271 (Nonfinancial corporate series) of *Fixed Reproducible Tangible Wealth in the United States, 1925–89*, published by the Bureau of Economic Analysis of the U.S. Department of Commerce, January 1993. The series for black median income was acquired from the Bureau of the Census, U.S. Department of Commerce, in constant dollars; it was converted to current dollars using the consumer price index reported in the annual *Economic Report of the President*. The number of adults by year is taken as the number of persons of age twenty and over, a series reported in the same publication. The data on composition of wealth of the wealthiest one-half of one percent of the population are reported in "Estimation of household net worth using model-based and design-based weights: Evidence from the 1989 Survey of Consumer Finance," by Arthur Kennickell and R. Louise Woodburn, Federal Reserve Board, April 1992 (unpublished working paper).

Notes

Introduction

1. Pareto-efficiency or Pareto-optimality is the economist's central concept of economic efficiency. An allocation of commodities or resources to individuals and firms is Pareto-efficient if there is no other feasible allocation of those commodities and resources that would render at least some individuals better off in terms of welfare and no individual worse off. The welfare of each individual is measured in terms of his own conception of welfare, as embodied in his utility function. (Utility functions are discussed in §8.) If an allocation is Pareto-efficient, then there is no waste, in the sense that the only way to render some people better off is to make some others worse off. Pareto-efficiency is a desirable property of an economic allocation, although it is not sufficient to render an allocation good from a social viewpoint, as it involves no assessment of the justice of the distribution. In a two-person economy, the allocation in which I receive all the goods and you none is Pareto-efficient, so long as I am not satiated.

2. An economic system is said to be in equilibrium if all persons and firms are simultaneously taking those actions which maximize their individual welfares or profits, subject to whatever constraints they face, and if all markets clear. Depending upon the precise nature of the economic system in question, this

definition may be framed in more specialized terms. In this essay, for example, I refer to "Walrasian" equilibrium, "Lange" equilibrium, and "Nash" equilibrium. These concepts describe precisely what economic equilibrium consists in according to the particular economic models discussed by Léon Walras, Oskar Lange, and John Nash, respectively. Economists also use these terms to describe equilibria in models which they view as having descended from the work of Walras, Lange, or Nash, even if these models show little resemblance to the original ones.

§1 *What socialists want*

1. See Elster (1985, pp. 82–92) for a discussion of self-realization in Marx, and Elster (1986) for a more general discussion, respectively.
2. Rawls (1971, p. 426).
3. C. B. MacPherson (1973, p. 4) defines democracy as equal self-realization among citizens. I think this embeds too much into the notion of democracy.
4. Arguments that justice entails equality of opportunity rather than equality of outcome are developed by Richard Arneson (1989, 1990) and G. A. Cohen (1989, 1990). I have tried to describe concretely how a society might institute equality of opportunity in Roemer (1993a).
5. I ignore a fine point here, the distinction between equality and the result of a *maximin* objective. (In economics, a maximin allocation is the allocation of resources which maximizes, over all feasible allocations, the welfare of the individual who is worst off. It may be that all allocations which yield equal welfare for all individuals make the worst-off person worse off than he would be at a maximin allocation. This may happen, for instance, because of deleterious incentive effects of the high rates of taxation that would be necessary to achieve complete equality. In these cases, most egalitarians would advocate the maximin allocation over any allocation achieving complete equality.)

With respect to opportunity for self-realization and welfare, I advocate choosing those social institutions which maximize opportunity for those who will have the *least* opportunity. It is not obvious, however, whether one should advocate the promotion of "maximin" opportunity for political influence or the goal of equal political influence at a maximum level, because political influence should probably be defined largely, though not entirely, in relative terms. Social status is a good similar to political influence in this respect: if everyone has equal social status, is it meaningful to speak about the level of that status?

6. Why advocate only equality of opportunity for social status, rather than equality of social status? It would be impossible to have the latter: criminals, for example, will necessarily have lower social status than others in a society. The society I claim socialists want should label people as criminals only if those who disobey the laws of their own accord, in the sense that they had the same real opportunities in life as those who chose to abide by the law. For a more precise discussion of how a society might equalize real opportunity, see Roemer (1993a).

7. See Roemer (1982, 1985).

8. See Adam Przeworski (1985).

§2 *Public ownership*

1. See, for contrasting positions on this question, Allen Wood (1972), who argues the latter view, and Norman Geras (1986), who argues the former.

2. In contrast to the political approach I take here, Joaquim Silvestre and I have taken a normative approach to public ownership, by asking what economic allocation arguably respects the public's ownership of an asset and the private ownership by individuals of their labor and other goods. We describe four allocation mechanisms, each of which has desirable properties. See Roemer (1989) and Roemer and Silvestre (1993).

3. Futures markets include insurance markets. Markets do not exist which would enable firms to purchase insurance against the possibility that, when a large investment, such as the build-

ing of a new plant, is completed, the demand for the firm's product may have fallen precipitously as a consequence of a general economic recession. Markets like this one would have to exist for investment levels to be socially optimal. An example of a positive externality associated with investment is development of new skills among the workers involved. The value of these skills to society will exceed their value to the original investor, which implies that the investment, on this account, will occur at a suboptimal level.

4. Public goods (such as clean air) and public bads (such as polluted air) are public because their *consumption* is, by nature, public; for example, clean air is a public good whereas a meal is a private good. Markets do not give rise to efficient quantities of public goods. Consequently, their production is often regulated by law, which is to say, by the political process. There is no necessary relationship between private goods and private ownership or public goods and public ownership, which is to say that both private and public goods can be produced by privately or publicly owned firms. Nevertheless, the government tends to be more involved in the production of public goods than private goods, because of the inadequacy of private markets in dealing with such goods.

5. This sentence might be taken to imply that I support immigration restrictions to guard against threats to public culture. I believe, however, that the inequality in access to resources which is determined by one's birthplace is morally arbitrary and ethically indefensible, and therefore I support much more liberal immigration laws than we have. Selling citizenships, in the presence of imperfect capital markets, would probably not alleviate the injustice (by virtue of resource inequality) inherent in the distribution of birthplaces, because the poorest would not be able to purchase citizenship in richer countries at market prices.

6. "Social-democratic" property is private property subject to taxation and regulation of various kinds.

§3 *The long term and the short term*

1. Mises (1947, p. 124). I thank Robin Blackburn for this quotation.
2. For an opposite view, that the Communists held back the popular struggle, see Adam Westoby (1981).
3. See Cohen (1989, 1990a) and Arneson (1989, 1990).
4. See Rawls (1971), Dworkin (1981), Sen (1985), Barry (1989), and Nagel (1991).
5. Some may doubt that socialists should be satisfied with the kind of egalitarianism that left-liberal political philosophers endorse. There are distinctions between socialist egalitarianism and Rawlsian egalitarianism: see Cohen (1992), who argues that Rawls allows incentive payments that a socialist egalitarian would disallow. But, as Brian Barry (1973, p. 166) wrote: "As I see it, then, the significance of *A Theory of Justice* is as a statement of liberalism which isolates its crucial features by making private property in the means of production, distribution, and exchange a contingent matter rather than an essential part of the doctrine and introduces a principle of distribution which could, suitably interpreted and with certain factual assumptions, have egalitarian implications. If socialism is identified with public ownership or with equality, then this form of liberalism is compatible with socialism."

§4 *A brief history of the idea of market socialism*

1. For an excellent history of market-socialist ideas within the socialist political movement, see the panoramic treatment of Blackburn (1992).
2. The marginal cost of production at a given level of production is the instantaneous rate at which costs increase as production increases from that level. Economic efficiency requires that the price of output be equated to its marginal cost.
3. A production process is characterized by constant or decreasing returns to scale if expanding all the inputs by a given factor will expand output by no more than that factor. Increasing returns

hold when expanding all the inputs by a given factor increases output by more than that factor.

4. It may seem obvious that *tâtonnement* should converge: if prices rise when demand exceeds supply, and fall when supply exceeds demand, why don't prices stabilize where supply equals demand? This makes sense if there is only one market; but with thousands of markets, the adjustment of prices on each market affects the disequilibrium condition on others, because demand for each good depends on the prices of many other goods. It thus becomes apparent that there is no guarantee that all prices can simultaneously stabilize all markets. In fact, the work of Debreu and Sonnenschein shows that it is exceedingly unlikely that the *tâtonnement* process converges in an economy with many markets. Economic theory still has no rigorous explanation for how prices can converge to provide a simultaneous equilibrium in all markets.

5. I phrase this criticism in the conditional mode because what Hayek in fact criticized was the proposal to allocate directly investment funds to firms, which differs from having firms choose how much to borrow from state banks at specified interest rates. See §12.

6. A firm's or a family's budget constraint is an expression of the fact that its choices in production or consumption are limited by its budget. A budget constraint is "soft" if it can be altered by negotiation with authorities in control of resources.

§5 *Why the centrally planned economies failed*

1. T. Boone Pickens, the U.S. corporate raider, relates how he purchased 25 percent of the stock of a Japanese firm with the aim of taking over its management and streamlining its operations. He was allowed one meeting with management: after that, his calls went unanswered. There were no shareholder meetings. He sought redress through the courts to have his say in corporate policy but was stonewalled. After two years, in disgust, he sold his interest in the firm. (*Washington Post*, April 28, 1991, p. C1.)

2. All figures are taken from Abram Bergson (1971).

3. See, for example, Burawoy and Lukacs (1985), who argue that workers in Hungarian factories worked as hard as U.S. workers.

4. Rent-seeking is the attempt to alter the distribution of resources or goods in one's own favor. This activity generally is costly and is to be contrasted with the productive activity of creating more resources or goods. Economists often view rent-seeking as socially wasteful, as resources are spent in altering who gets certain goods instead of in producing more of those goods. Rent-seeking, however, is not necessarily wasteful; if we judge the redistribution of goods in question to be a social improvement, or if the process of rent-seeking gives rise to a different productive outcome, we would not think it a waste. If, for example, the stock market is essentially a gambling casino, as Keynes once wrote, then the activity of trade on the stock exchange would be classed as harmful rent-seeking; if, on the other hand, the stock market is a mechanism for allocating investment funds to their socially optimal use, then, although stock-market trade would still constitute rent-seeking in the sense defined, it would not be judged a net waste to society.

5. I specify innovation as a "generic, multisectoral phenomenon" here because of the example of the defense and space industries, in which innovation has been dramatic and almost entirely engendered by demands of the state, rather than by competition, in both the Soviet Union and the United States. Moreover, there have been substantial spillovers from innovations in these industries to the rest of the economy. Because of the importance of this example, one can reasonably doubt whether market competition is necessary to produce technological innovation as a generic phenomenon in an economy. As I've said, I will here assume, conservatively, that it is.

§7 Public bads and the distribution of profits

1. The public bad in this case is apartheid, if investment in such firms extends its life.

2. This assumes that we have a social-welfare function. A social-welfare function provides a way of aggregating the welfares experienced by individuals into one number, which is taken to be the welfare of society. Many economists are wary of such aggregations, on the grounds that it is difficult to arrive at a scientific basis for comparing the welfares experienced by different individuals, and hence to aggregate their welfares in a salient way. For some discussions of this problem, see Elster and Roemer (1991).

3. This is so even if the rich cannot escape exposure to the public bad, as indeed they often can. Recall the rationalization of social-republican property in the prevention of local public bads, in §2.

4. A simple model will serve to illustrate the phenomenon I have described. Consider a population of persons each of whom has a utility function $u(x,z)$, where x is a private good produced by a firm that also produces the public bad z. (Think of z as an amount of pollution, for example.) Each person receives a wage $w(z)$ and a fraction θ of the firm's profits, $\pi(z)$; profits and wages depend on the level of pollution that the firm is allowed to emit. Assume that both wages and profits increase as a function of the amount of pollutant allowed, but at a decreasing rate:

$$w'(z) > 0, \qquad w''(z) < 0$$
$$\pi'(z) > 0, \qquad \pi''(z) < 0$$

We will study the optimal level of pollution from the point of view of a person who owns share θ of the firm and hence receives that share of its profits. For example, let $u(x,z) = x - bz^2$. Then the person's problem is to choose (x,z) to maximize $x - bz^2$ subject to $x = w(z) + \theta\pi(z)$. (The constraint just says that the person's consumption of the private good is the sum of his wage and profit income, which we may think of as paid in units of the private good.) By substituting the expression for x into the objective function and setting the first derivative with respect to z of the objective equal to zero, we obtain the first-order condition:

$$w'(z) + \theta\pi'(z) = 2bz$$

This equation expresses a relationship between the optimal value of z and the share θ. To see how the optimal z changes with θ, differentiate the equation above implicitly with respect to θ, which yields:

$$w'' \frac{dz}{d\theta} + \theta\pi'' \frac{dz}{d\theta} + \pi' = 2b \frac{dz}{d\theta}$$

or

$$\frac{dz}{d\theta} = \frac{-\pi'}{w'' + \theta\pi'' - 2b}$$

It follows from our assumptions on the signs of the derivatives of w and π that

$$\frac{dz}{d\theta} > 0$$

Thus, the larger the person's share of the firm, the larger the person's optimal level of pollution. In an economy described by this simple model, large shareholders would try to influence the political process—if that is the process that prescribes the level of z—to legislate allowances for higher permitted levels of pollution by the firm.

5. *Sacramento Bee*, April 16, 1991, p. G1.
6. See also Roemer (1993b).

§8 *A model of a market-socialist economy*

1. Why doesn't the firm simply maximize expected profits? Because this is a model with incomplete asset markets, in general,

and in such a world, maximizing expected profits is not necessarily in the interest of all shareholders. (This is a well-known fact about economies with incomplete markets.)

2. I have proposed and studied elsewhere models in which the rich can influence the outcome of elections in which they are in a small minority, through campaign spending and electoral propaganda. See Roemer (in press, 1992c).

3. The utility function of every agent is $u(x_0, x_2, z) = x_0^{.5} + x_2^{.5} - z$, where x_0 and x_2 are consumption of the good at dates 0 and 2 and z is consumption of the public bad at date 2. There are 95 poor agents, each endowed with 10 units of the good at date 0, and 5 rich agents, each endowed with 300 units of the good. There are two firms and three states of the world. The production function for firm j in state s is $g_s^j(x,z) = a_s^j x^{c_j} z^{(1-c_j)}$, where $c_1 = .7$, $c_2 = .3$, $(a_1^1, a_2^1, a_3^1) = (5,13,30)$, and $(a_1^2, a_2^2, a_3^2) = (9,13,16)$.

4. One might argue that a political party representing the rich, and knowing Table 1, would advise the rich to reduce their influence in the political process! The rich would be better off abdicating, as it were. (For a discussion of the "abdication theory of the state" in Marx—why it is sometimes in the best interest of the bourgeoisie not to hold state power—see Elster (1985, pp. 411–422).) But if the influence of the rich in the political process is the aggregated result of the actions of many rich citizens not acting in concert, this may not be possible.

An interesting criticism of the model, as presented here, has been made by Samuel Bowles. I have taken the value of λ to be exogenously given. But the degrees of political influence of the rich and the poor should be endogenous to the model. Indeed, citizens spend resources in order to gain political influence, and these expenditures should be taken into account in making the comparison of the two politico-economic systems. If citizens spent much more in the market-socialist mechanism than in the capitalist one in "rent-seeking" (trying to influence the political process), that expense would lower welfare generally in market socialism and would count as a mark against it. This effect cannot be evaluated without proposing a theory for the determination of λ by the expenditure of resources.

5. In Czechoslovakia, 11.5 million citizens each purchased, for 1,000 crowns, a voucher booklet in January 1992, with which stock of formerly state-owned enterprises would eventually become purchasable. Most of these vouchers were invested in private "investment trust funds" that sprang up, offering people a guaranteed return of ten times their original investment (10,000 crowns) in one year's time. At this writing (March 1993), it is reported that well over half of those vouchers have now been invested in nine large investment trust funds, which are privately owned by a small number of people. In turn, these nine funds control just under 50 percent of the shares of 1,500 newly privatized Czech firms. The largest investment trust fund, the Harvard Capital and Consulting Company, is owned by one man, Viktor Kozeny. (See "Keeping in Czech," *The Financial Times*, 17 February 1993.) Rarely, if ever, in the history of capitalism has the concentration of capital occurred so rapidly!

6. It is perhaps important to emphasize that I am not recommending that stock markets be introduced immediately—that is, during the transition phase—in the former Communist states. Jean Tirole (1992) argues effectively that, in the initial "noisy" phase, one should not use stock prices to monitor firm management. The proposed economic mechanism of this section is intended as one operating in a stable politico-economic environment.

§9 *The efficiency of firms under market socialism*

1. One could view the different "states of the world" at date 2 as the consequences of different futures with regard to technological innovation. The point, however, is that those possible futures are not affected, in the model, by the kind of property relations that are adopted.

2. This might appear to differ from the structure of the coupon economy in §8, where investors finance the firm directly. But,

by the Modigliani-Miller theorem, the equilibria in those models are isomorphic to equilibria in models where the banks finance firms, and citizens deposit funds in banks. The general-equilibrium model of §8 did not address the monitoring question, and so the distinction between bank financing and individual investor financing was of no import. More generally, the Modigliani-Miller theorem holds only in a world in which monitoring of firms is not affected by the financial structure of the firm.

3. I have not specified the control and ownership structure of banks in the market-socialist proposal. I will here suppose that they are publicly owned in the sense that their profits go in large part directly to the state treasury. Their managers, however, would be hired on a competitive managerial labor market, as described below.

4. See Corbett and Mayer (1991) and Franks and Mayer (1990).

§11 *State intervention in the economy*

1. Smeeding, O'Higgens, and Rainwater (1990) report that the percentage of persons who are poor after taxes and transfers is 4.8 in Norway, 5.0 in Sweden, 6.0 in West Germany, 8.8 in the United Kingdom, 12.1 in Canada, and 16.9 in the United States. These numbers are roughly rank-correlated with the extent of welfare-state provisions in these countries.

2. See Nicholas Barr (1992) for a sophisticated justification of the welfare state via the economic theory of uncertainty and asymmetric information.

3. A second reason such insurance is not privately provided is that the risks co-vary—all firms in the population would suffer the bad state simultaneously, bankrupting the insurance company. This is why the government, also, cannot provide such insurance in an open economy.

4. The Coase theorem asserts that, as long as property rights are well defined, no final allocation can be Pareto-nonoptimal, for even if some markets do not exist, coalitions of agents can always form and negotiate to Pareto-optimal allocations.

§12 *A digression on investment planning*

1. A full discussion, complete with models and theorems, is available in Ortuño, Roemer, and Silvestre (1993); a short summary is Roemer and Silvestre (1993).
2. This is, in reality, a poor assumption: but we have made a number of simplifying assumptions to make the analysis of the problem tractable. One hopes, in such cases, that complexifying the model will not disturb too much the general character of the results.
3. The pattern of investment may be undesirable for the reasons discussed in §11. The alert reader will note that none of these reasons in fact apply to the model just described: there are no public goods, no externalities, and futures markets exist. Nevertheless, our concern in this section is to study the extent to which the investment vector of an economy can be altered by government intervention, and to this end we have elected to study a model which is as simple as possible—in particular, one in which there are no public goods, externalities, etc.
4. But see the Drèze (1989) proposal for how an economy with firms that maximize net income per worker can be led to a Pareto-efficient equilibrium.

§13 *Socialism and democracy*

1. See Schmitter and Karl (1992) for definitions of democracy, and Riker (1982) for general skepticism concerning the feasibility of democracy.
2. A more cynical view maintains that the war had no important economic aims but was only a means by which President Bush could save his reputation after his imprudent excessive flirtation with Saddam Hussein. Even were this so, the point I have made applies to genuine imperialist wars.
3. For models, evidence, and reference to other literature, see Reich (1981) and Roemer (1979).
4. Recall Tibor Scitovsky's (1976) view that happiness comes from a change to something different, not a stably good situation.

5. Hashimoto (1992) reports that, in Japan, the Honda training program for workers involves them studying manuals. When Honda set up its U.S. plant, it discovered that workers were unable to learn by reading manuals.

6. To put the argument in the language of §7, we would say that, after a point, the *lack* of public education is a profit-increasing public bad.

7. The four countries that contribute the greatest fraction of their GNP to official development assistance are Norway, Sweden, the Netherlands, and Denmark. Each of these contributes at least 0.94 percent of its GNP. Among the 18 countries constituting the Development Assistance Committee of the OECD, the United States ranks last, contributing only 0.15 percent of its GNP (OECD, 1990).

§14 *Criticisms of market socialism from the left*

1. A step could be better in two senses: it could put us on a path that would reach our long-term goal earlier, or it could itself realize more equality than market socialism does. There is no reason to think that the social design which is optimal in the first sense is also optimal in the second. I will not pursue this problem further.

2. For the modern statement of this philosophy, see Nozick (1974).

3. On this point, see G. A. Cohen (1990b).

4. There is an important exception to this claim: the distribution of jobs between the employed and unemployed has an arbitrary element; there are, that is, unemployed workers who may be just as qualified as employed ones but who cannot find work. Several modern theories of unemployment will generate this result. My claim in this part of the sentence is that, with competitive labor markets, there cannot be too much variation in the distribution of wage earnings among the employed workforce, given the distribution of skills and other parameters of the economic environment.

5. See Murrell (1992) for a characterization of conservatism not

as a liberal political philosophy but as a one-step-at-a-time approach to changing the politico-economic mechanism.

6. In addition to Weisskopf (1993), Fleurbaey (1993), and Drèze (1993), see Bowles and Gintis (1993).

7. This paragraph simply asserts that the situation where all firms are labor-managed may be a Pareto-suboptimal Nash equilibrium.

Appendix: The value of the coupon dividend in the United States

1. I am grateful to Fred Block for advice in the preparation of this Appendix.

2. In the national accounts, π^{cap} is computed by subtracting taxable depreciation from the firm's net income. But taxable depreciation differs from economic depreciation. The capital consumption allowance is the difference between depreciation reported to the IRS and estimated economic depreciation. Adding it to profits in the accounting equation is supposed to give a figure which is closer to actual economic profits.

3. It can be argued, of course, that the liberalized depreciation laws reflected an increase in the rate of technological change, and therefore a decrease in the useful economic lifetime of plant and equipment.

References

Andvig, J. C. 1992. "Transitions to Market Economies." Working paper, Norwegian Institute of International Affairs, Oslo.

Arneson, R. 1989. "Equality and Equal Opportunity for Welfare." *Philosophical Studies*, 56: 77–93.

——— 1990. "Liberalism, Distributive Subjectivism, and Equal Opportunity for Welfare." *Philosophy & Public Affairs*, 19: 158–194.

Arrow, K., and L. Hurwicz. 1960. "Decentralization and Computation in Resource Allocation." In *Essays in Economics and Econometrics*, pp. 34–104. Chapel Hill: University of North Carolina Press.

Bardhan, P. 1993. "On Tackling the Soft Budget Constraint in Market Socialism." In *Market Socialism: The Current Debate*, ed. P. Bardhan and J. Roemer. New York: Oxford University Press.

Bardhan, P., and J. Roemer. 1992. "Market Socialism: A Case for Rejuvenation." *Journal of Economic Perspectives*, 6: 101–116.

——— (eds.). 1993. *Market Socialism: The Current Debate*. New York: Oxford University Press.

Barone, E. 1935. "The Ministry of Production in the Collectivist State." In *Collectivist Economic Planning*, ed. F. A. Hayek. London: George Routledge & Sons.

Barr, N. 1992. "Economic Theory and the Welfare State: A Survey and Interpretation." *Journal of Economic Literature*, 30: 741–803.

Barry, B. 1973. *The Liberal Theory of Justice*. New York: Oxford University Press.

—— 1989. *Theories of Justice*, vol. 1. Berkeley: University of California Press.

Ben-Ner, A., and E. Neuberger. 1990. "The Feasibility of Planned Market Systems: The Yugoslav Visible Hand and Negotiated Planning." *Journal of Comparative Economics*, 14: 768–790.

Bergson, A. 1971. "Development under Two Systems: Comparative Productivity and Growth since 1950." *World Politics*, 23: 579–607.

Blackburn, R. 1991. "Fin de Siècle: Socialism after the Crash." *New Left Review*, 185: 5–66.

Block, F. 1977. "The Ruling Class Does Not Rule: Notes on the Marxist Theory of the State." *Socialist Revolution*, 33 (May–June): 6–28.

—— 1992. "Capitalism without Class Power." *Politics and Society*, 20: 277–303.

Bowles, S., and H. Gintis. 1986. *Democracy and Capitalism*. New York: Basic Books.

—— 1993. "The Democratic Firm: An Agency-Theoretic Formulation." In *Democracy and Markets: Problems of Participation and Efficiency*, ed. S. Bowles, H. Gintis, and B. Gustaffson. New York: Cambridge University Press.

Bowles, S., H. Gintis, and B. Gustaffson. 1993. *Democracy and Markets: Problems of Participation and Efficiency*. New York: Cambridge University Press.

Brus, W. 1972. *The Market in a Socialist Economy*. London: Routledge & Kegan Paul.

Burawoy, M., and J. Lukacs. 1985. "Mythologies of Work: A Comparison of Firms in State Socialism and Advanced Capitalism." *American Sociological Review*, 50: 723–737.

Cohen, G. A. 1989. "On the Currency of Egalitarian Justice." *Ethics*, 99: 906–944.

—— 1990a. "Equality of What? On Welfare, Goods and Capabilities." *Recherches Economiques de Louvain*, 56: 357–382.

—— 1990b. "Marxism and Contemporary Political Philosophy,

or: Why Nozick Exercises Some Marxists More Than He Does Any Egalitarian Liberal." *Canadian Journal of Philosophy*, Supplementary Volume 16: 363–367.

———— 1991. "The Future of a Disillusion." *New Left Review*, 190 (November–December): 5–22.

———— 1992. "Incentives, Inequality, and Community." In *The Tanner Lectures on Human Values*, vol. 13, ed. G. B. Peterson. Salt Lake City: University of Utah Press.

Cohen, J., and J. Rogers. 1983. *On Democracy: Toward a Transformation of American Society*. New York and London: Penguin.

———— 1993. "Associative Democracy." In *Market Socialism: The Current Debate*, ed. P. Bardhan and J. Roemer. New York: Oxford University Press.

Corbett, J., and C. Mayer. 1991. "Financial Reform in Eastern Europe: Progress with the Wrong Model." *Oxford Review of Economic Policy*, 7: 55–75.

Debreu, G. 1974. "Excess Demand Functions." *Journal of Mathematical Economics*, 1: 15–23.

Dewatripont, M., and E. Maskin. 1993. "Centralization of Credit and Long-Term Investment." In *Market Socialism: The Current Debate*, ed. P. Bardhan and J. Roemer. New York: Oxford University Press.

Diamond, D. 1991. "Monitoring and Reputation: The Choice between Bank Loans and Directly Placed Debt." *Journal of Political Economy*, 99: 689–721.

Drèze, J. 1989. *Labour Management, Contracts, and Capital Markets*. Oxford: Basil Blackwell.

———— 1993. "Self-management and Economic Theory: Efficiency, Finance, and Employment" In *Market Socialism: The Current Debate*, ed. P. Bardhan and J. Roemer. New York: Oxford University Press.

Dworkin, R. 1981. "What Is Equality? Part 2: Equality of Resources." *Philosophy and Public Affairs*, 10: 283–345.

Elster, J. 1985. *Making Sense of Marx*. New York: Cambridge University Press.

———— 1986. "Self-Realization in Work and Politics: The Marxist

Conception of the Good Life." *Social Philosophy & Policy*, 3: 97–126.

Elster, J., and J. E. Roemer. 1991. *Interpersonal Comparisons of Well-Being*. Cambridge: Cambridge University Press.

Fleurbaey, M. 1993. "An Egalitarian Democratic Private Ownership Economy." In *Market Socialism: The Current Debate*, ed. P. Bardhan and J. Roemer. New York: Oxford University Press.

Franks, J., and C. Mayer. 1990. "Corporate Ownership and Corporate Control: A Study of France, Germany, and the UK." *Economic Policy*, 10: 189–231.

Geras, N. 1986. *Literature of Revolution: Essays on Marxism*. London: Verso.

Hashimoto, M. 1992. "Employment-Based Training in Japanese Firms in Japan and in the United States: Experiences of Automobile Manufacturers." Working Paper, Department of Economics, Ohio State University, Columbus.

Hayek, F. A. 1935. "The Nature and History of the Problem." In *Collectivist Economic Planning*, ed. F. A. Hayek. London: George Routledge & Sons.

——— 1940. "Socialist Calculation: The Competitive 'Solution.'" *Economica*, 7: 125–149.

Hirschman, A. O. 1982. *Shifting Involvements: Private Interests and Public Action*. Princeton, N.J.: Princeton University Press.

Jowitt, K. 1991. *The New World Disorder*. Berkeley: University of California Press.

Kornai, J. 1992. *The Socialist System: The Political Economy of Communism*. Princeton, N.J.: Princeton University Press.

——— 1993. "Market Socialism Revisited." In *Market Socialism: The Current Debate*, ed. P. Bardhan and J. Roemer. New York: Oxford University Press.

Lange, O. [1936] 1956. "On the Economic Theory of Socialism." In *On the Economic Theory of Socialism*, ed. B. Lippincott. Minneapolis: University of Minnesota Press.

Lydall, H. 1989. *Yugoslavia in Crisis*. Oxford: Clarendon Press.

Major, I. 1992. "The Decay of Command Economies." Manuscript, Hungarian Institute of Economics, Budapest.

MacPherson, C. B. 1973. *Democratic Theory*. Oxford: Clarendon Press.

Mises, L. von. 1947. *Planned Chaos*. Irving-on-Hudson, N.Y.: Foundation for Economic Education.

Moene, K., and M. Wallerstein. 1993. "What's Wrong with Social Democracy?" In *Market Socialism: The Current Debate*, ed. P. Bardhan and J. Roemer. New York: Oxford University Press.

Murrell, P. 1992. "Conservative Political Philosophy and the Strategy of Economic Transition." *East European Politics and Societies*, 6: 3–16.

Murrell, P., and M. Olson. 1991. "The Devolution of Centrally Planned Economies." *Journal of Comparative Economics*, 15: 239–265.

Nagel, T. 1991. *Equality and Partiality*. New York: Oxford University Press.

Nove, A. 1983. *The Economics of Feasible Socialism*. London: George Allen and Unwin.

Nozick, R. 1974. *Anarchy, State, and Utopia*. New York: Basic Books.

Organization for Economic Cooperation and Development (OECD). 1990. *Development Cooperation Efforts and Policies of Members of the Development Assistance Committee*. Paris: OECD.

Ortuño, I., J. Roemer, and J. Silvestre. 1993. "Investment Planning in Market Socialism." In *Democracy and Markets: Problems of Participation and Efficiency*, ed. S. Bowles, B. Gustaffson, and H. Gintis. New York: Cambridge University Press.

Pollin, R. 1993. "Public Credit Allocation through the Federal Reserve: Why It Is Needed; How It Should Be Done." In *Transforming the U.S. Financial System: Equity and Efficiency for the 21st Century*, ed. G. Dymski, G. Epstein, and R. Pollin. Armonk, N.Y.: M. E. Sharpe.

Porter, M. 1992. *Capital Choices: Changing the Way America Invests in Industry*. Washington, D.C.: Council on Competitiveness.

Przeworski, A. 1985. "Material Interests, Class Compromise, and the Transition to Socialism." In *Analytical Marxism*, ed. J. E. Roemer. New York: Cambridge University Press.

—— 1985. *Capitalism and Social Democracy*. New York: Cambridge University Press.

—— 1992. "The NeoLiberal Fallacy." *Journal of Democracy*, 3: 45–59.

Rawls, J. 1971. *A Theory of Justice*. Cambridge, Mass.: Harvard University Press.

Reich, M. 1981. *Racial Inequality*. Princeton, N.J.: Princeton University Press.

Reigg, N. 1978. "The Role of Fiscal and Monetary Policies in Taiwan's Economic Development." Ph.D. thesis, University of Connecticut, Storrs.

Riker, W. H. [1982] 1988. *Liberalism against Populism*. Prospect Heights, Ill.: Waveland Press.

Quinzii, M. 1992. *Increasing Returns and Economic Efficiency*. New York: Oxford University Press.

Roemer, J. 1979. "Divide and Conquer: Microfoundations of a Marxian Theory of Wage Discrimination." *Bell Journal of Economics*, 10: 695–705.

—— 1982. "Property Rights versus Surplus Value in Marxian Exploitation." *Philosophy and Public Affairs*, 11: 281–313.

—— 1985. "Should Marxists Be Interested in Exploitation?" In *Analytical Marxism*, ed. J. E. Roemer. New York: Cambridge University Press.

—— 1989. "A Public Ownership Resolution of the Tragedy of the Commons." *Social Philosophy & Policy*, 6: 74–92.

—— 1992a. "Can There Be Socialism after Communism?" *Politics and Society*, 20: 261–276.

—— 1992b. "A Proposal for Denationalization of the State Sector When Pollution Is an Issue." Working Paper No. 404, Department of Economics, University of California, Davis.

—— 1992c. "The Use of Campaign Finance to Influence Voters' Beliefs." Working Paper No. 405, Department of Economics, University of California, Davis.

——— 1993a. "A Pragmatic Theory of Responsibility for the Egalitarian Planner." *Philosophy and Public Affairs*, 22: 146–166.

——— 1993b. "Would Economic Democracy Decrease the Amounts of Public Bads?" *Scandinavian Journal of Economics*, 95: 227–238.

——— In press. "The Strategic Role of Party Ideology When Voters Are Uncertain about How the Economy Works." *American Political Science Review*.

Roemer, J., and J. Silvestre. 1992. "A Motivation for Investment Subsidies." Manuscript, University of California, Davis.

——— 1993a. "Investment Planning in Market Socialism." In *Market Socialism: The Current Debate*, ed. P. Bardhan and J. Roemer. New York: Oxford University Press.

——— 1993b. "The Proportional Solution for Economies with Both Private and Public Ownership." *Journal of Economic Theory*, 59: 426–444.

Sah, R., and M. Weitzman. 1991. "A Proposal for Using Incentive Pre-Commitments in Public Enterprise Funding." *World Development*, 19: 595–603.

Schmitter, P., and T. L. Karl. 1991. "What Democracy Is . . . And Is Not." *Journal of Democracy*, 2: 75–88.

Scitovsky, T. 1976. *The Joyless Economy: An Inquiry into Human Satisfaction and Consumer Dissatisfaction*. New York: Oxford University Press.

Sen, A. 1985. *Commodities and Capabilities*. Amsterdam: North-Holland.

Silvestre, J. In press. "Public Ownership and Public Goods." *Revista Española de Economía*.

Simon, William. 1991. "Social-Republican Property." *UCLA Law Review*, pp. 1335–1413.

Smeeding, T., M. O'Higgens, and L. Rainwater. 1990. *Poverty, Inequality, and Income Distribution in Comparative Perspective*. Washington, D.C.: The Urban Institute.

Sonnenschein, H. 1973. "Do Walras' Identity and Continuity Characterize the Class of Community Excess Demand Functions?" *Journal of Economic Theory*, 6: 404–410.

Stiglitz, J. 1985. "Credit Markets and the Control of Capital." *Journal of Money, Credit, and Banking*, 17: 133–152.

Tirole, J. 1992. "Ownership and Incentives in a Transition Economy," Institut d'Economie Industrielle, Document de Travail 10, University of Toulouse.

Wade, R. 1990. *Governing the Market.* Princeton, N.J.: Princeton University Press.

Weisskopf, T. 1993. "A Democratic-Enterprise-Based Socialism." In *Market Socialism: The Current Debate*, ed. P. Bardhan and J. Roemer. New York: Oxford University Press.

Westoby, A. 1981. *Communism since World War II.* New York: St. Martin's Press.

Wood, A. 1972. "The Marxian Critique of Justice." *Philosophy and Public Affairs*, 1.

Index